CULTURES OF THE WORLD

Bangladesh

Mariam Whyte & Yong Jui Lin

mc **Marshall Cavendish**
Benchmark
New York

PICTURE CREDITS

Cover: © Adam Buchanan/Danita Delimont

Albert Moldvay/National Geographic Image Collection: 9 • Audrius Tomonis: 135 • Christopher Pillitz/Getty Images: 78 • Craig Pershouse/Lonely Planet Images: 1 • Dave Saunders/ Art Directors & Trip: 107, 114 • David Greedy/Lonely Planet Images: 44, 52, 76, 99, 100, 110, 112, 116, 123, 127 • Deshakalyan Chowdhury/ AFP/Getty Images: 12 • Dick Durrance II/ National Geographic/ Getty Images: 75 • Farjana K. Godhuly/ Getty Images: 54, 120 • Francis Tan JY: 130 • Hutchison/Eye Ubiquitous: 20, 67, 106 • Hutchison: 17, 21, 95 • James Balog/Getty Images: 58 • James P. Blair/National Geographic Image Collection: 70 • Jason Laure: 7, 8, 10, 34, 86, 88 • Jerry Galea/ Lonely Planet Images: 5, 128 • Junko Kimura/Getty Images: 50 • Justin Guariglia/ National Geographic Image Collection: 85 • Karen Kasmanski/National Geographic Image Collection: 57 • Khan Godhuly/AFP/Getty Images: 118 • Manan Vatsyayana/ AFP/ Getty Images: 97 • Michael Steele/Getty Images: 113 • Munir Uz Zaman/AFP/Getty Images: 31, 36, 47, 96, 103 • Noah Seelam/AFP/Getty Images: 119 • photolibrary: 13, 15, 16, 19, 40, 41, 48, 51, 56, 62, 63, 64, 65, 66, 71, 72, 79, 80, 81, 90, 91, 93, 101, 122, 125, 126, 129, 131 • Richard I'Anson/Lonely Planet Images: 2, 6, 18, 42, 73, 83, 98, 124 • Shobbir Mia/AFP/Getty Images: 22 • Still Pix: 87, 115 • Strdel/ AFP/ Getty Images: 77 • Tim Laman/ National Geographic Image Collection: 46 • Tony Wheeler/Lonely Planet Images: 32, 82 • Topham Picturepoint: 11, 14, 25, 27, 28, 30, 33, 43, 102 • Trip: 24, 35, 39, 45, 84, 92, 94, 111, 117

PRECEDING PAGE

Bangladeshi woman with her son.

Publisher (U.S.): Michelle Bisson
Editors: Deborah Grahame, Stephanie Pee
Copyreader: Tara Koellhoffer
Designer: Lock Hong Liang
Cover picture researcher: Connie Gardner
Picture researcher: Thomas Khoo

Marshall Cavendish Benchmark
99 White Plains Road
Tarrytown, NY 10591
Web site: www.marshallcavendish.us

© Times Media Private Limited 1997
© Marshall Cavendish International (Asia) Private Limited 2010
® "Cultures of the World" is a registered trademark of Times Publishing Limited.

Originated and designed by Marshall Cavendish International (Asia) Private Limited
A member of Times Publishing Limited

Marshall Cavendish is a trademark of Times Publishing Limited.

All Internet sites were correct and accurate at the time of printing. All monetary figures in this publication are in U.S. dollars.

Library of Congress Cataloging-in-Publication Data
Whyte, Mariam.
  Bangladesh / by Mariam Whyte and Yong Jui Lin.
    p. cm. — (Cultures of the world)
  Includes bibliographical references and index.
  ISBN 978-0-7614-4475-6
  1. Bangladesh—Juvenile literature. I. Yong, Jui Lin. II. Title.
  DS393.4.W49 2010
  954.92--dc22   2009003184

Printed in China
7 6 5 4 3 2 1

CONTENTS

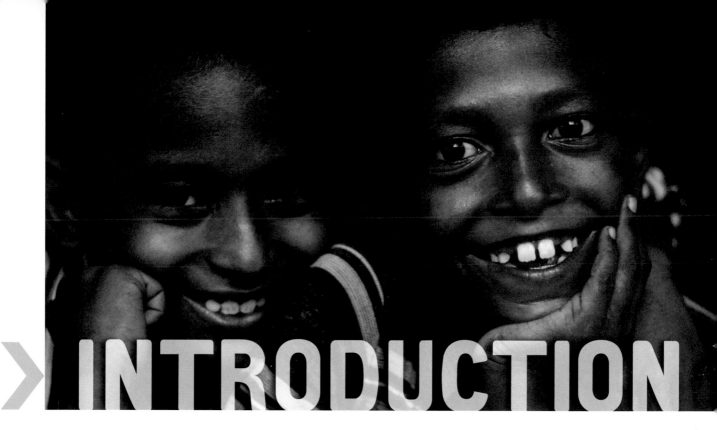

INTRODUCTION

BANGLADESH IS ONE of the world's youngest nations. Historically it has been part of India and has been reborn twice, once as East Pakistan and again as Bangladesh. Bangladeshis fought for many years to gain their independence, first to protect their religion, then to protect their language. Today the country is still fighting, at present to achieve a government that can turn the nation's aspirations into reality.

Bangladesh is overpopulated and poor, and the journey to economic stability has been compounded by political turmoil. Frequent torrential floods create even more problems for the country. The people of Bangladesh are, however, enormously proud of their country, and these struggles have not dampened their spirits. Instead, they have worked to enrich their culture and to instill a strong national identity.

Established in 1971, Bangladesh has endured famines, natural disasters, widespread poverty, and political turmoil. The restoration of democracy in 1991 has been followed by relative stability and economic progress. Significant progress in human development in the areas of literacy, gender equality in schooling, and reduction of population growth has also been made.

GEOGRAPHY

Boats on the Meghna River between crops
of deep-water rice and water hyacinths.

CHAPTER 1

BANGLADESH IS LOCATED IN southern asia. It is bordered by Burma (Myanmar) to the southeast and India to the west, north, and northeast. Of its total land boundary of 2,637 miles (4,246 km), about 120 miles (193 km) of border are shared with Burma and the rest with India. Bangladesh also has about 360 miles (580 km) of coastline overlooking the Bay of Bengal.

Bangladesh is mainly flat, connected and drained by a system of rivers. It is prone to flooding, which provides rich alluvial soil that is good for agriculture, but can also bring devastation.

The country covers 55,598 square miles (144,000 square km), an area slightly smaller than the state of Wisconsin. However, due to the overwhelming flatness of the land and the heavy monsoons that blow through each year, bringing heavy rain, a large portion of the country is permanently flooded.

WEB OF RIVERS

An extensive and intricate web of rivers is Bangladesh's most significant geographical feature.

Right: The road to Jessore in western Bangladesh.

The rivers have been a major factor in shaping life and culture in Bangladesh. With over 118 inches (300 cm) of snow and rainfall annually, the eastern Himalayas to the north of Bangladesh provide a major water supply to the Ganges/Brahmaputra/Meghna river systems that empty into the Bay of Bengal.

The rivers bring down the rich alluvial soil that forms the Ganges Delta, and they provide the main means of transportation throughout the country. Rivers are also a source of hydroelectric power, a notable example being the Karnaphuli River in the southeast. Because the rivers are subject to constant and often rapid change, Bangladesh's topography never remains the same for long.

A classic example of this occurred in 1787 when the Tista River experienced massive flooding. Waters were diverted eastward, where they met and

A boat plies one of Bangladesh's many rivers.

reinforced the Brahmaputra River. The swollen Brahmaputra then cut into a minor stream and by the early 1800s the minor stream had become the river's main watercourse, now called the Jamuna. The Brahmaputra, now a considerably smaller river below the juncture with the Jamuna, still flows along the old course.

CHITTAGONG HILL TRACTS

Bangladesh has almost no mountains. The highest elevations in the country are in the southeast, in the Chittagong Hill Tracts. Here some hills rise to more than 2,000 feet (600 m), but the area is not typical of Bangladesh's topography.

Bangladesh's Chittagong Hill Tracts area is just a small section of a much larger mountain range that stretches from western Burma to the eastern Himalayas in China. The steep jungle hills, ravines, and cliffs that are found here are a stark contrast to the flat plains in the rest of Bangladesh.

Mist rising above the Chittagong Hill Tracts presents a breathtaking sight.

Bangladesh's highest peak, the Keokradong (3,041 feet/927 m), is found in the Chittagong Hill Tracts in the southeast of the country.

Unlike the rest of Bangladesh, the Chittagong Hill Tracts area has a relatively low population density. These hills are home to the indigenous peoples collectively known as the Jumma.

The Sylhet region in the northeast is Bangladesh's only other hilly area. Some parts of these hills, which range from 100 to 800 feet (30 to 240 m) high, are covered with forests of bamboo.

SUNDARBANS

The Sundarbans are a massive area of littoral mangrove and jungle found in the southwest of the country on the Ganges Delta, bordering the Bay of Bengal. Covering an area of about 3,860 square miles (10,000 square km), this belt of forest is the largest of its type in the world, and stretches over Indian and Bangladeshi territory: 40 percent in India, 60 percent in Bangladesh.

A ferry on a river in the Sundarbans, an area that has been a national park since 1984.

Almost half of the Sundarbans lies under water. The low-lying alluvial islands, mudbanks, forested areas, and sandy dunes and beaches that form the coast characterize the land above water. These are divided by an intricate system of interconnecting waterways. Tidal waves sweep the area occasionally and, coupled with tidal movements and erosion that affect the area, constantly change and reform much of the land. The Sundarbans were severely damaged by a cyclone in November 2007.

KAPTAI LAKE

Kaptai Lake is one of the world's largest man-made lakes, covering about 263 square miles (680 square km). During the rainy season the lake can swell to about 400 square miles (1,036 square km). The lake was constructed during the building of the Karnaphuli hydroelectric plant in 1961.

Situated roughly in the center of the Chittagong Hills, the dam displaced more than 100,000 tribal people who lost their livelihood when much of the area's arable land was flooded. The Karnaphuli hydroelectric plant, however, remains an important source of power for Bangladesh today.

Kaptai Lake has been developed into a leisure destination.

THE LONGEST BEACH IN THE WORLD

The beaches along Bangladesh's southeast coast near Cox's Bazar are the longest continuous stretch of beaches in the world, extending over 74 miles (120 km). At high tide the beaches are over 650 feet (200 m) wide; at low tide this width can extend to 1,300 feet (400 m).

Running parallel to the beaches for the entire length of the coast are the forests of the Chittagong Hill Tracts, making the area one of the most picturesque in all of Bangladesh.

THE BENGALI SEASONAL CYCLE

The traditional Bengali year has six "seasons" of two months each that are related to the growing of cash crops. The New Year begins on April 14 in the month of Boishakh *("bow-ee-SHAKH").*

• *The months of* Boishakh *and* Joishtho *("JOSH-toh"), mid-April to mid-June, are the season of* Grishsho *("GRISH-show"), a warm summer period when rice and jute are cultivated.*

• *During* Borsha *("BOR-shah"), the months of* Ashar *("AH-shar") and* Shrabon *("SRA-bon"), mid-June to mid-August, it rains incessantly and crops are harvested.*

• Sharad *("shah-RUHD") marks the end of the monsoon rains in the months of* Bhadro *("BAH-drow") and* Ashshin *("AH-sheen"), mid-August to mid-October. Jute is collected and processed at this time.*

• Hemonto *("HEH-mon-tow"), the months of* Kartik *("KAR-tik") and* Ogrohayon *("oh-gro-HOY-on"), mid-October to mid-December, begins a period of cooler weather when vegetable crops are planted.*

• Sheet *("sheet") is the coolest season of the year. During the two months of* Sheet, Poush *("po-SH") and* Magh *("MAHG"), mid-December to mid-February, fresh fruit and vegetables are abundant.*

• Falgoon *("fahl-GOON") and* Choitro *("CHOY-trow") are the last two months of the year, mid-February to mid-April. This is the season of* Boshonto *("boh-SHON-tow"), when the last of the* Sheet *crops are harvested and flowers blossom.*

CLIMATE

Bangladesh has a tropical monsoon climate. The year is divided roughly into three seasons: a hot, humid buildup from March to June; a rainy period from late May to mid-October; and a cooler, dry season from October to March. About 6 percent of the total land area is permanently flooded, but when the heavy monsoon rains fall, up to two-thirds of the land is deluged.

During the dry season, the land is parched and barren, and drought and famine are major concerns. Farmers anxiously await the first monsoon rains, although this anticipation is coupled with a fear that the rains will be unsatisfactory. If the rains are too light they will be ineffective. If they are too heavy they could destroy the crops. The average annual rainfall varies between 55 inches (140 cm) in the dry Rajshahi area and over 200 inches (508 cm) in the Sylhet region.

Devastation left in the wake of the worst cyclone in Bangladesh's history.

FLORA AND FAUNA

Bangladesh enjoys a rich and varied flora and fauna. Tropical fruit such as mangoes, bananas, papayas, coconuts, and jackfruit grow abundantly throughout the country. The Chittagong Hills and the Sundarbans are covered with thick forests that yield valuable timber, some of which is processed to make newsprint.

Animal life is also abundant. Bangladesh has more than 100 species of mammals, 628 species of birds (including migratory ones), more than 100 species of reptiles, and more than 200 species of marine and freshwater fish. The country's most famous animal is the Bengal tiger. Elephants, as well as several species of deer, including the barking deer, sambar, and spotted deer, live in the forests of the Chittagong Hills. Other animals found in Bangladesh include turtles, monkeys, gibbons, crocodiles, lizards, and snakes.

The jackfruit is a popular fruit in Bangladesh.

The Bengal tiger is so important to the people of Bangladesh that Bangladesh is often referred to as "The Land of the Bengal Tiger," and the tiger is recognized as a national symbol.

The tigers mainly live in the tropical jungles of the Sundarbans in the southwest of Bangladesh, but they may also be found in parts of Nepal, India, Bhutan, and Burma. Growing up to 10 feet (3 m) in length and weighing up to 500 pounds (225 kg), the Bengal tiger eats medium to large prey such as pigs and deer. The tigers have also been known to attack humans from time to time.

The tigers usually live for about 15 years in the wild; they live slightly longer in a controlled environment such as a zoo. These majestic animals were once populous, but because their pelts are highly prized and the people of some cultures believe that their bones have medicinal value, the Bengal tigers have themselves become prey and now number fewer than 3,000 in the wild. Another 300 live in zoos around the world.

Besides the Bengal tiger, other surviving subspecies of tigers include the Indochinese tiger, the Siberian tiger, the South China tiger, and the Sumatran tiger. Of these the South China tiger is the most critically endangered, with fewer than 30 living in the wild.

MAJOR CITIES

DHAKA Formerly known as Dacca, Dhaka is the capital of Bangladesh and its largest city. It is located almost exactly in the country's geographic center, in the region of the Ganges and Brahmaputra river deltas, and has a population of approximately 11 million, spread over approximately 565 square miles (1,464 square km).

Founded in the 10th century, Dhaka has since seen many changes. Under the Mogul Empire, it was the capital of Bengal province from 1660 to 1704. Dhaka then became a trading center for British, French, and Dutch interests before it came under British rule in 1765. In 1905 it was made the capital of Bengal, and then became the capital of East Pakistan in 1956. The city suffered widespread damage during the 1971 war for independence. When Bangladesh won its independence from Pakistan, the name of the city was changed from the anglicized version, Dacca, to the Bengali name of Dhaka.

The capital city of Bangladesh, Dhaka.

Scientists believe stripes help tigers hide from their prey. Like human fingerprints, a tiger's stripes are unique—no two tigers have the same pattern of stripes. This distinctive pattern of stripes is on the tiger's skin.

Dhaka is the commercial heart of Bangladesh. The city has a moderate-sized middle-class population, driving the market for modern consumer and luxury goods. For much of recent history, Dhaka was characterized by roadside markets and small shops that sold a wide variety of goods. Recent years have seen the widespread construction of shopping malls, multiplexes, hotels, and restaurants attracting Dhaka's growing middle-class and wealthy residents.

The city has historically attracted large number of migrant workers. Hawkers, peddlers, small shops, rickshaw transportation, roadside vendors, and stalls employ a large segment of the population—rickshaw drivers alone number as many as 400,000. This is the largest number of rickshaws for any city in the world. Half the workforce is employed in household and unorganized labor, while about 800,000 work in the textile industry. Even so, unemployment remains high, at 23 percent.

Many rickshaws jam the streets of Dhaka.

Dhaka is known the world over as the city of mosques; the Muslim festivals of Eid ul-Fitr and Eid ul-Adha witness widespread celebrations, with large numbers of Muslims attending prayers in mosques across the city.

CHITTAGONG The second-largest city and the chief port of Bangladesh, Chittagong is about 9 miles (15 km) up the Karnaphuli River from the Bay of Bengal. About 4 million people live there. Chittagong is surrounded by hills, making it one of Bangladesh's most scenic cities. Being the country's primary port, Chittagong is the main route for almost all of Bangladesh's imports and exports. Its harbor contains extensively developed port facilities.

KHULNA Located along the banks of the Rupsa and Bhairab rivers, Khulna is Bangladesh's third-largest city, with a population of nearly 1.4 million. Because of its strategic location, only 30 miles (48 km) from the port of Mongla, Khulna is a port city as well. Khulna is also famous for its seafood and coconut industries.

A little shop in Forest Lake Park in Chittagong.

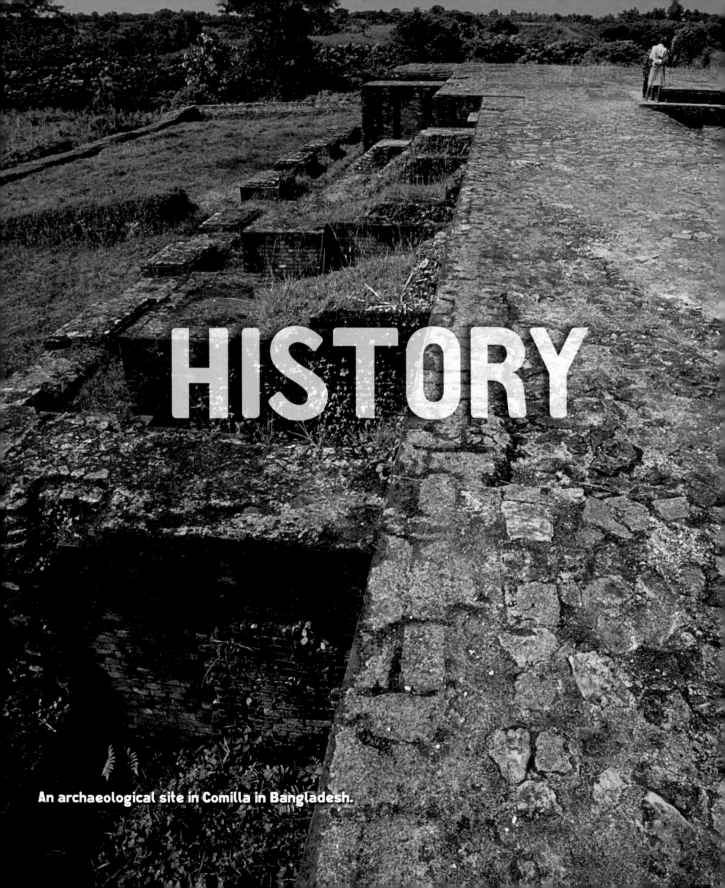

HISTORY

An archaeological site in Comilla in Bangladesh.

B

ANGLADESH IS A NEW NATION in a political sense, having been created in its present form less than 30 years ago after the 1971 war for independence. Its culture and civilization, however, go much further back in history, spanning over 3,000 years.

EARLY CIVILIZATION

The first inhabitants of the region in prehistoric times were an Austro-Asian race of people. Then there was settlement by the Dravidians, the Aryans, and the Mongolians.

The Martyrs' Memorial commemorates those who died in the 1971 war for independence.

Bangladesh dates back to at least the fourth century B.C. Buddhism was introduced by Asoka, and it was embraced by many. Subsequently the region was taken over by Muslim invaders and most of the population converted to Islam. Eventually Bangladesh was colonized by the British. Bangladeshis began to agitate for independence, which they gained in 1972.

The earliest references to areas in Bangladesh can be found in the ancient texts of the Ramayana and the Mahabharata. But these references are mythological rather than historical. Reliable accounts became available only early in the fourth century B.C. It was around this time that the historians of Alexander the Great recorded accounts of a powerful civilization inhabiting the lower Ganges region, the Gangaridai. According to one of these historians, Diodorus, Alexander supposedly decided not to undertake an expedition against the Gangaridai after being "deterred by the multitude of their elephants." Greek geographer Ptolemy, who lived in the second century A.D., also made references in his works that can be traced to modern-day Bangladesh.

From the fourth to the second century B.C., the region was dominated by the Mauryan Empire, of which Asoka was the last major emperor. Little is known about the next few centuries until the rise of the Gupta Empire

Bangladeshi boys examine a scale model of Kantanagar temple, an 18th-century Hindu temple, at the Concorde Heritage Park, the country's first park featuring scale models of the nation's most famous monuments.

ASOKA

Asoka reigned from 265 B.C. to 238 B.C. and was one of the greatest and noblest rulers the Indian subcontinent has known. It was his patronage of Buddhism that enabled the then-fledgling religion to spread throughout India and eventually to East Asia.

His conquest of Kalinga on India's east coast in 261 B.C. marked a turning point in his life. He was sickened by the death and suffering he caused, and it was the last war he ever fought. Asoka embraced Buddhism and put the humane and benevolent ideals of Buddhism into practice, including the appointment of "Officers of Righteousness" who saw that the local authorities promoted welfare and happiness among his subjects. His famous edicts, carved on rocks, in caves, and on specially erected pillars, still survive today.

in the fourth century A.D. The Guptas ruled the region until the dynasty's collapse in the seventh century and the rise of the first independent king of Bengal, Sasanka (ruled 600—625). The Gupta period was notable for its artistic development, much of which originated in the Bengal region. Gupta art later influenced the people of Southeast Asia. Renowned Chinese pilgrim Hsien Tsang, who visited the Bengal region between 639 and 645, wrote of the flourishing Buddhist states he found there.

In the eighth century, following a century of chaos in Bengal, a warrior named Gopala was elected to the throne in an attempt to impose some semblance of order. Gopala reigned from 750 to 770. He founded the Pala dynasty, which brought prosperity and stable government to the region for more than four centuries. Its patronage nurtured the arts and sheltered the remnants of the Buddhists in the Indian subcontinent where Hinduism was becoming a powerful force. The Palas were the last powerful Buddhist monarchs on the subcontinent. They also established diplomatic relations with the kingdom of Srivijaya, which controlled much of the Indonesian archipelago.

The Palas were succeeded by the Sena dynasty at the end of the 11th century. The Senas ruled Bengal until the early 13th century. Under the Senas, Hinduism replaced Buddhism as the main object of royal patronage.

Alexander the Great was one of the greatest conquerors in history. From his base in Macedonia, he overthrew the powerful Persian Empire, subdued Egypt, and invaded India.

ARRIVAL OF ISLAM

In the early 13th century, invaders from Afghanistan and central Asia, who were sweeping across the northern regions of the Indian subcontinent and had established the Mamluk dynasty in Delhi, overthrew the Sena dynasty and converted most of the population to Islam. Thus began the Turkic domination of the region. Waves of Turks, Arabs, Pakhtuns, Persians, and others began migrating to Bengal, and a period of vigorous cultural and architectural achievement took place.

In 1556 Akbar acceded to the throne of the Mughal Empire and began enlarging its borders. By 1576 Bengal had become a province within the empire. European traders—first the Portuguese, and later the Dutch and British—began to arrive. By 1616 the Portuguese had established a post at Dhaka. The decline of the Mughal Empire began after the death of its last

One of the surviving mosques of Lalbagh Fort in Dhaka's Old City.

great emperor, Aurangzeb, in 1707. In the chaos that followed, British traders began to take over the region and the Indian subcontinent.

EARLY INDEPENDENCE MOVEMENTS

It is the events leading up to and during the 20th century that resulted in the establishment of the nation of Bangladesh. British colonialists continually tried to strengthen their administrative control of east India, absorbing lands east of Calcutta, including the remaining portion of Bengal and the Ganges River valley. By 1859 the British had dominion of India from the Indus River in the west to Bengal in the east.

Under Lord Curzon, a British statesman, Bengal was divided into two separate provinces, West and East Bengal, in 1905. The partition provoked loud protests among the population that eventually led to the reunification

Lord Curzon (*left*), viceroy of India from 1898 to 1905, partitioned Bengal in 1905. Curzon was the youngest viceroy in the history of India.

of Bengal. The Muslim and Hindu factions of India, tired of being subordinate to the British, began to press for greater independence from the British government.

The Hindu Indian National Congress primarily led the movement for independence. The Muslim faction became concerned about Hindu domination, and in 1906 they formed the All-India Muslim League. The league aimed to ensure proper consideration of Muslim needs. The congress and the league coordinated their efforts in 1913, with the same fundamental goal in mind: self-government for India within the British Empire. The Muslims were not satisfied, however, that their religious, economic, and political needs were being adequately protected. The next two decades were fraught with bitter conflicts between the Hindu and Muslim communities.

BANGLADESH AS PAKISTAN

In the 1930s the idea of a separate Muslim state arose as the solution to the conflicts. This state, eventually named Pakistan, was to be specifically dedicated to the religious ideals of Islam. Finally, after several years of debate, in 1947 India was given independence and Pakistan was created. Bengal was divided into East Bengal and West Bengal. West Bengal became part of the new Indian nation, while East Bengal became East Pakistan.

It appeared that the quest for autonomy was over for the Bengali Muslims. However, almost from the moment Pakistan was formed, conflicts arose between the east and the west sectors of Pakistan. The first major difficulty was over the issue of language. The structure of Pakistan had left its political center, and thus its ruling elite, in the west, while the majority of the population lived in the east.

Mohammad Ali Jinnah, one of the Muslim leaders who led the move to form Pakistan, declared in a speech in 1948 that Urdu must become the official language of Pakistan. Curiously Urdu was not the native tongue of any of the people of Pakistan, although some people could understand it reasonably well. Only a little over 0.4 percent of the population spoke Urdu, as opposed to over 56 percent who spoke Bengali.

This seemingly illogical choice of Urdu as the national language was explained by suggesting that Urdu had a closer affinity to Arabic and Persian. Since Pakistan existed to accommodate Muslims, who derived their historical traditions from Mogul rule, Urdu was considered the appropriate choice of language. Urdu was coincidentally the language that was spoken by most of the politicians and was regarded as the elite language of Pakistan.

There was a strong feeling, particularly in East Pakistan, that its political leaders were not satisfactorily representing all of Pakistan, but instead were only protecting their personal interests. Taking into consideration Pakistan's unique geopolitical and socioeconomic structures, its diversity in culture, and the enormous geographic distance between the east and the west, it was imperative to its survival that democratic power be given to both parts of the country on an equitable basis. The obvious neglect and exploitation of most of Pakistan by an elite class caused a division between the east and west, giving little chance for any national unity.

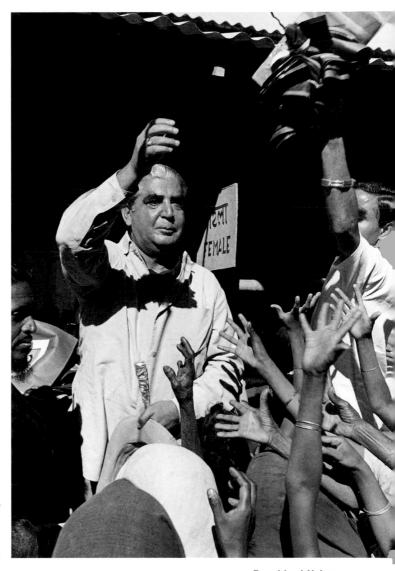

President Yahya Khan's actions in 1971 sparked off the war for independence.

WAR OF INDEPENDENCE

The Awami League, a Dhaka-based nationalist party, won the national elections in 1970, taking 167 of the 169 seats allotted to East Pakistan. This left the Awami League with an overall majority in the 313-member Pakistan National Assembly.

The president of Pakistan, Yahya Khan, dissatisfied with the results, postponed the opening of the National Assembly. Riots and strikes broke out in East Pakistan. Sheikh Mujibur Rahman, leader of the Awami League, then proclaimed the independence of Bangladesh on March 26, 1971.

Civil war immediately erupted, and Sheikh Mujibur Rahman was arrested and taken to West Pakistan. By April 1971 Pakistani soldiers had occupied all major towns. Still resistance continued. In November a major offensive by Mukhti Bahini (Liberation Army of East Bengal) guerrillas forced some 10 million people to flee into neighboring India. India subsequently declared war on Pakistan on December 4, 1971, joining the conflict. The combined forces of the Indian army, local guerrillas, and the civilian population eventually forced Pakistan's surrender on December 16, 1971.

In January 1972 Bangladesh was officially declared an independent nation. Sheikh Mujibur Rahman, who had been released by Pakistan's new president, Zulfikar Ali Bhutto, became the country's first prime minister.

General Mohammed Ershad ruled Bangladesh from 1982 to 1990. He joined the army in 1953 and became Chief of Army Staff General in 1978 before seizing power in 1982.

A NEW NATION

The early years of Bangladesh's independence saw famine, martial law, military coups, and political assassinations. Floods in 1974 devastated the fragile Bangladeshi economy and led to famine and a cholera epidemic that left thousands dead. Sheikh Mujibur Rahman, who had banned all political parties except the Awami League and become the country's president, was assassinated in August 1975.

JUMMA HISTORY

The area of the Chittagong Hill Tracts was first colonized by the British in 1860, marking the first time in their history that the local tribes belonged to a state. The annexation was primarily a military strategy to enable the British to station troops on the eastern borders to defend themselves against intruders.

The next few years were a period of growing legal and commercial "Bengalization," with many Bengali businessmen converging on the region. As a result, the British government proclaimed itself the protector of tribal rights and implemented an exclusion policy that forbade Bengalis from dealing with the tribespeople in business or political matters. This policy worked, slowing down the process of Bengalization. But it also effectively isolated the Hill Tracts from the rest of Bengal and made the tribespeople dependent on the British.

The colonizers claimed ownership of the land and distributed prime portions to European entrepreneurs. They encouraged outsiders—other than Bengalis—to settle in the hills, forcing the tribespeople to relocate. The policy of exclusion had effectively deprived the Hill Tracts people of economic or political power, and, consequently, they took no part in decisions that directly affected them. The pressure of increasing population, overcultivation of the land, and the lack of nonagricultural employment eventually plunged the hill people into an economic crisis.

The hill tribes endured this situation until the 1970s, when Bangladesh was formed. The war for independence left Bangladesh overpopulated and in chronic poverty, and the idea to settle in the "empty" and "unutilized" Hill Tracts surfaced. The hill people were also regarded as less cultured, and it was felt that the Bengali migrants would help civilize them in the Bengali tradition. The hill people did not respond well to what they perceived as an invasion of their lands. They united as one group, calling themselves the Jummas, and retaliated with open rebellion.

The Bangladeshi government sent in the army and full-scale guerrilla warfare ensued. The conflict caused thousands of deaths and led to a mass exodus to refugee camps in India and Burma. However, in 1997, peace talks between the leaders of the guerrilla movement and the new Bangladeshi government resulted in an agreement to end the conflict. The tension in the hills has not entirely eased, but the prospect of reconciliation provides hope for a peaceful future.

Disgruntled Bangladeshis held a torchlight procession in support of a strike in 1992.

In the coups and counter-coups that followed, Chief of Army Staff General Ziaur Rahman took power. Political parties were legalized again, and in 1978 the extremely popular general Ziaur Rahman ("Zia") won Bangladesh's first direct presidential election. Parliamentary elections followed in 1979, with Zia's Bangladesh Nationalist Party winning 49 percent of the total votes and 207 seats in the 300-seat parliament. Martial law was lifted and the state of emergency revoked. Zia went on to forge relationships with the West and the Islamic countries of the Middle East. In 1981, however, he was assassinated, and the government returned to a military dictatorship.

General Mohammad Ershad later seized power in a bloodless coup in March 1982 and placed the country under martial law. He became the prime minister and in December 1983 declared himself president. Although he won the presidential election in 1986, which was boycotted by both the Awami League and the Bangladesh Nationalist Party, there was growing opposition to his rule.

In 1990 General Ershad was finally forced to resign by opposition groups and democracy was reestablished. Following elections in February 1991, General Zia's widow, Begum Khaleda Zia, was named prime minister.

After a time general dissatisfaction with the government grew and when she was reelected in 1996, voters questioned the legitimacy and integrity of the election. Once again Bangladeshis went on strike and rallied against the reelected government. Zia eventually resigned. New elections were held in June 1996 and a coalition government, headed by the daughter of Sheikh Mujibur Rahman, Sheikh Hasina Wajed of the Awami League, was elected.

The Awami League lost to the Bangladesh Nationalist Party again in 2001. Concern has grown about religious extremism in the traditionally moderate and tolerant country, which found apparent form in a string of bomb attacks in August 2005. The government, which long denied that it had a problem with militants, has outlawed two fringe Islamic organizations.

In January 11, 2007, following widespread violence, a caretaker government was appointed to run the next general election. The country had suffered from extensive corruption, disorder, and political violence. The new caretaker government has made it a priority to root out corruption from all levels of government. The caretaker government claims to be paving the way for free and fair elections, which were held on December 29, 2008.

Voters queue up outside a polling station in Dhaka.

GOVERNMENT

The national assembly building in Dhaka.

THE PEOPLE'S REPUBLIC OF Bangladesh has seen many changes in its government since it was first established. The progression toward the form of government that exists today has been fraught with numerous political assassinations, martial law, and instances of corruption.

The constitution drawn up in 1972 created a parliamentary government, and promoted nationalism, secularism, socialism, and democracy as its basic principles. In 1975 this form of government was replaced by a presidential one in which the president held near-dictatorial power.

A coup in 1981 marked the beginning of a 10-year military regime. In 1991 this dictatorship was overthrown and the government returned to the parliamentary system, with the election victory of Begum Khaleda Zia's Bangladesh Nationalist Party.

THE FIRST LEADER

Sheikh Mujibur Rahman, a founding member of the Awami League, was the

Right: Sheik Mujibur Rahman (1920–75) was Bangladesh's first prime minister.

33

first prime minister of the independent sovereign nation of Bangladesh. He was named president at the first proclamation of Bangladeshi independence, but for almost the entire duration of the war, Mujib, as he was called, was imprisoned in West Pakistan.

He was charged and convicted of treason and sentenced to death. Upon the surrender of the Pakistani forces he was released and allowed to return to Bangladesh, where he assumed the presidency. Only two days later he vacated that office to become prime minister.

Mujib pushed through a new constitution in which the nation would be led by a prime minister who would be appointed by the president and approved by a unicameral (single house) parliament. Over the first years of his leadership, Mujib did little to improve the country's social and economic problems. Nevertheless he was reelected at the first national elections in 1973. His popularity decreased considerably after that as flooding, famine,

Sheik Mujibur Rahman is warmly received in Dhaka after his release from Pakistan in 1972.

and rising crime made it apparent that Mujib could not effectively resolve the country's problems.

In 1975 Mujib changed the constitution to make himself president for five years, and gave himself full executive powers. He then proclaimed Bangladesh a one-party state, effectively discarding the parliament and making himself dictator. Later that same year Mujib, his wife, and three sons were assassinated by a group of young army officers.

STRUCTURE OF GOVERNMENT

Bangladesh has a republican government. The head of state is the president, who is elected by popular vote. The head of government is the prime minister, who leads a cabinet of ministers. A prime minister is a head of government, not of state. All countries have both a head of state and a head of government, though the offices may be combined. The head of government is the one who actually leads the cabinet. The second pattern is president as head of state and prime minister as head of government. This is the most common pattern worldwide; examples include Germany

The parliament building in Dhaka.

The president is elected for a term of five years and is eligible for reelection. The current president, Iajuddin Ahmed, has been in office since 2002.

and France. These ministerial positions were formerly filled by presidential appointments, but now all positions are only given to candidates elected by popular vote.

The House of the People, the legislative assembly, is a unicameral parliament with 300 seats. Legislative bills are passed by a majority vote of the members of parliament. A bill that has been passed by parliament goes to the president for approval. If the president gives his approval it becomes law. If not, it is returned to parliament for further debate. If it is passed for the second time it will become law, regardless of presidential approval.

THE PRIME MINISTER

Dr. Fakhruddin Ahmed was appointed as the chief advisor (head of the government) of the nonparty interim caretaker government of Bangladesh on January 12, 2007, amid chaos in Bangladeshi politics. Dr. Ahmed is a noted Bangladeshi economist, civil servant, and a former governor of the Bangladesh

The current prime minister of Bangladesh, Sheik Hasina Wazed.

Bank, the country's central bank. Since his government is an interim one and he was not elected by popular vote to the position, he is not known officially as the prime minister of Bangladesh.

While he was governor of Bangladesh Bank, Dr. Ahmed introduced wide-ranging reforms. Financial sector reforms included stronger corporate governance measures at the board level and also on internal policies, processes, and structures within the banking industry and for nonbank financial institutions. Other significant reforms undertaken during his tenure included strengthening the capacity of floating the exchange rate with minimal volatility, introducing interest rate flexibility and bringing down the interest rate substantially. This helped bring about a significant increase in industrial investment, introducing major corporate governance measures for the first time in the Bangladeshi corporate sector and making the Bangladesh Bank an effective regulator and enforcer. The reforms implemented during Dr. Ahmed's tenure contributed to financial sector growth and stability in a major way.

Dr. Ahmed is respected on both sides of the sharp political divide in Bangladesh and is credited with bringing an end to the anarchy that had threatened to sweep the troubled nation. Because Bangladesh is widely perceived as one of the most corrupt countries, one of the most dramatic aspects of Ahmed's rule is his campaign to stamp out corruption, especially within the government. So far more than 160 senior politicians, top civil servants, and security officials have been arrested on suspicion of graft and other economic crimes. Former ministers from the two main political parties, including former prime ministers Sheikh Hasina and Khaleda Zia, have also been caught.

MILITARY

The three arms of the Bangladeshi defense force are the army, the navy, and the air force. They were established in 1972, soon after the war for independence. Originally all defense forces consisted mainly of deserters from the Pakistani forces, and most of their weapons and equipment were stolen or captured, or were spoils of the war.

"We want to form the government after the elections on the basis of national consensus. We want to build a society free from terrorism, corruption, and poverty. We want to fully equip the nation with the ability to enter the 21st century along with other developed countries of the world." —Sheikh Hasina Wajed, campaign speech, May 10, 1996

After years of unfulfilled promises that elections would be held "soon," Bangladesh finally held a general election in 1996—only the second free election in 25 years of self-government. Voters all over the country walked, bicycled, or rowed boats to the polls and waited in long lines for the opportunity to cast their votes. On the ballots, parties and candidates were represented by symbols to help the large proportion of illiterate voters.

Even this election, which was generally regarded as being free and fair, was difficult. At least 20 people were killed during the month-long campaign preceding it. Some 40,000 soldiers and 400,000 police and security forces were called in to reinstate order among the rival political activist groups. On the day of the election itself, two more people were killed in gun battles outside two different polling stations.

The army now has around 110,000 troops, the navy has about 9,000 troops, and the air force has approximately 6,500 troops. Service in the defense forces is voluntary and is not restricted by religious or ethnic affiliation. All male citizens over the age of 16 are eligible for voluntary military service and may become officers at 17 years of age. Bangladesh's military equipment includes Russian- and Chinese-built tanks.

Bangladesh also has a paramilitary force of about 67,000, called the "Bangladesh Rifles," who are border guards. They are known to the Bangladeshi people as the Vigilant Sentinels of Our National Frontier.

POLICE

The Bangladeshi police force has been essentially rebuilt since 1972. The war for independence rendered the police system of East Pakistan completely ineffective, with most of its members defecting to join the Mukhti Bahini (the Liberation Army) or simply deserting.

At the top of the police hierarchy is the armed police. This is a highly trained, elite unit responsible for stopping violence and public disorder that is beyond the strength of the local police force. The armed police also operate an intelligence wing.

The Shanti Bahini (Peace Army) is an army-based guerrilla force in the Chittagong Hills. It was established in 1973 as the armed wing of the Parbatya Chattagram Jana Sanghati Samity (PCJSS), a political front of the people of the Chittagong Hill Tracts. Members of the Shanti Bahini have been fighting with the Bangladeshi government for more than 20 years. They seek recognition of the rights of the tribal communities in the region. They abandoned militancy following the peace treaty signed by the government and the Shanti Bahini on December 2, 1997.

The general police force is administered by the inspector general. There are superintendents at the district level and inspectors at the subdistrict level. The local constabulary is the lowest rank in the police force and is integral to domestic security. The Bangladesh police also contribute to UN peacekeeping missions.

JUDICIARY

Government courts operate at regional, district, and subdistrict levels. Judges in these courts are appointed by the government. In addition, at the village level there is a form of magistrate court where disputes are initially taken.

These village courts are presided over by the local leader and two other judges, who are nominated by the disputing parties. Most cases are resolved in the village court, but in cases where one of the disputing parties wants another opinion, the case is taken to a government court of a higher level. If taken far enough, the case eventually reaches the Supreme Court. The Supreme Court consists of a chief justice and other judges who are appointed by the president.

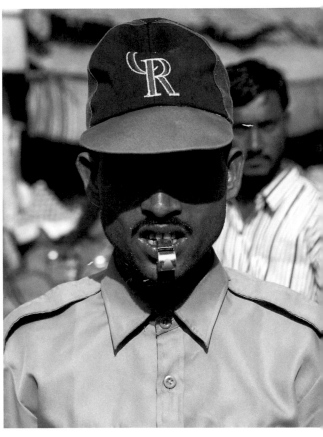

A traffic police officer in Sylhet.

ECONOMY

A woman selling snacks.

ACCORDING TO a 2007 International Monetary Fund (IMF) list, Bangladesh ranked as the 48th-largest economy in the world. Although it is one of the world's poorest and most densely populated countries, Bangladesh has made major strides to meet the food needs of its increasing population. Nonetheless an estimated 10 to 15 percent of the population faces serious nutritional risk.

Bangladesh's predominantly agricultural economy depends heavily on an erratic monsoon cycle. Although things are improving, the infrastructure is poorly developed and Bangladesh's industrial base is weak. The country's main endowments include its vast human resource base, rich agricultural land, relatively abundant water, and substantial reserves of natural gas.

THE WORKFORCE

In rural communities the work of women and men is strictly segregated,

Most Bangladeshis are engaged in the key industries of agriculture and manufacturing. More women are joining the workforce, a realm previously dominated by men.

Right: Children in rice fields.

with men working in the fields and women doing the household chores. This is not the case in the cities. A large proportion of urban men work as rickshaw drivers or laborers, while the better educated hold professional jobs.

Although most women in the workforce are self-employed or employed in low-skill jobs, their participation in high-skill and entrepreneurial jobs as well as policymaking bodies is on the rise. There also have been remarkable improvements in women's educational attainments. On the whole women's status in Bangladesh is improving at an astonishing rate.

AGRICULTURE

Agriculture is Bangladesh's most important economic sector. It accounts for about 19 percent of the country's gross domestic poduct (GDP) and provides employment to almost two-thirds of the working population. Some 20.8 million acres (8.44 million hectares) of land are under cultivation.

Most farms in Bangladesh are small; a quarter of the estimated 14 million farms are only half an acre (0.2 ha) or less. Half of the total farms are between

Farmers planting rice in their fields.

1 and 4 acres (between 0.4 and 1.6 ha). Most of the small farms are cultivated by the owners and their families and provide a subsistence living. The larger farms benefit from the use of technology and fertilizers and produce a surplus that is sold in markets. Their owners manage the farms and are considered the elite of rural society.

Bangladesh's major agricultural products are rice, jute, wheat, tea, cotton, tobacco, beef, milk, and poultry. Some food crops are grown chiefly for the domestic market, such as oilseeds, potatoes, sweet potatoes, sugarcane, and fruits such as bananas, jackfruit, mangoes, and pineapples. Jute and rice are the primary crops, but maize and vegetables are becoming more important.

Rice is harvested three times a year. The winter harvest in November/December is the most important one. It provides the best-quality grain and the biggest crop. Winter-harvested rice is grown mainly in the lowlands, with the sowing done in May. The summer harvest in August/September is the next most important harvest and is grown on comparatively higher

Drying rice in Cox's Bazar.

ground. Jute also grows well on the same land during the same period as rice, so farmers must decide which crop to plant, depending on how well each did the previous season. If the prospects look better for jute, farmers may choose to plant more jute at the expense of rice. The third and smallest type of rice crop grows mainly in low-lying marshy areas.

Tea plays a major role in the country's economy and is second only to jute as a money earner. The most important tea-growing regions are found in the east, in Sylhet and Chittagong. Thanks to improved production techniques and the use of better seeds, yields have increased dramatically over the last few decades.

Sugarcane has become an important cash crop, even though Bangladesh's climate and much of its land are not ideal for its cultivation. Rising domestic demand for sugar has ensured its continued popularity, despite the poor yields compared to other parts of the world.

Tobacco, another cash crop, is grown mainly in the north of the country. Rangpur is Bangladesh's leading tobacco-producing area. Tobacco's importance, however, has been declining as farmers favor other crops. Wheat, another minor crop, is grown mainly in the northern districts.

A girl walks through a tea plantation. Tea is one of Bangladesh's most important crops.

Jute, corchorus olitorius, grows up to 4 feet (1.2 m) tall and bears shiny green leaves and bright yellow flowers that form long seedpods. Jute is second only to cotton as the world's most productive and useful fiber. The plant has been grown in Bangladesh since ancient times, but exports of raw jute to the West began only in the 1790s. Jute can be made into garments, carpets, twine, footwear, paper, and ornaments. Its single largest use, however, is in sacks and burlap bags that are used to ship grain, flour, sugar, and other agricultural produce. The leaves also make a tasty addition to cooking.

Bangladesh is the world's leading producer of jute and jute products, and jute production plays a dominant role in the country's economy. There are more than 100 jute mills, jute textile mills, jute carpet mills, and jute twine mills, providing employment for thousands of Bangladeshis and bringing in a large proportion of national revenue.

Besides Bangladesh and India, jute is also grown in China and Brazil. Japan, Germany, and the United Kingdom are the world's largest importers of raw jute fiber.

The fibers of the jute plant are held together by a gummy material. Before the fibers can be extracted and used, the gum must be softened and removed. This is usually done by putting bundles of harvested jute stems in a pool of water for up to a month to allow bacteria to break down the gummy tissues.

FISHING

Fish, which makes up more than 80 percent of animal protein in the Bangladeshi diet, is also vital to the economy. The fish caught are mostly freshwater varieties, but overfishing has depleted stocks and ocean varieties are now increasingly common in the markets. Most people living in coastal communities make their living from fishing, and approximately 14 million people work at least part-time in the fishing industry. Fisheries contribute around 4.7 percent to Bangladesh's GDP and about 10 percent of annual export earnings.

Bangladesh also has several inland shrimp farms. The World Bank and the Asian Development Bank, as well as private investors, have financed projects to develop shrimp aquaculture by constructing new hatcheries and updating technology to increase the average yields.

Fishermen set traps to catch shrimp larvae in the river's current.

MINERALS

Bangladesh has large potential natural gas reserves and small reserves of coal and oil. Natural gas accounts for about 66 percent of the country's commercial energy consumption. Despite increasing production levels, Bangladesh has never been a net exporter of natural gas. Given the uncertain size of the country's natural gas reserves, the government has been reluctant to export natural gas and has instead focused on meeting current and future domestic energy needs.

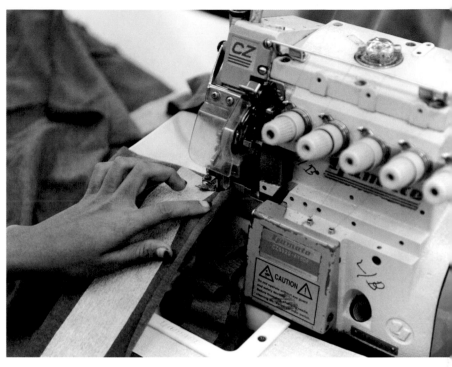

A factory worker operating machinery at a garment factory. Bangladesh is the largest exporter of clothing after China.

Bangladesh began commercial coal production in April 2003, and the government has recently promoted the development of coal to ease its reliance on natural gas for power generation. Bangladesh has 28 million barrels of oil reserves, and it produces 4,000 barrels of oil per day. However, it still remains an oil importer, as it consumes 91,000 barrels of oil per day.

MANUFACTURING

Manufacturing employs about 11 percent of the workforce and contributes about 28.7 percent of the country's GDP. Many new jobs—mostly for women—have been created by the country's dynamic private ready-made garment industry, which grew at double-digit rates through most of the 1990s. By the late 1990s about 1.5 million people, mostly women, were employed in the garments sector. During 2001 to 2002, export earnings from ready-made garments reached $3.125 million, representing 52 percent of Bangladesh's total exports.

Traffic congestion is common in Dhaka.

TRANSPORTATION

Bangladesh has a fairly extensive road system, with about 148,648 miles (239,226 km) of main roads and 14,121 miles (22,726 km) of paved secondary roads. There are three main crossings into Bangladesh from India: at Benopol-Haridispur on the Calcutta route, at Chilihari-Haldibari on the Darjeeling route, and at Tamabil-Dawki on the Shillong route. Prior to the 1950s there were several overland routes between the subcontinent and Burma, but these were closed for political reasons.

The streets of most major cities such as Dhaka are extremely congested, and driving a car or riding a motorcycle can be very dangerous. Road accidents are common and a crowd quickly gathers when one occurs. Buses provide a cheap mode of transportation for Bangladeshis. In the cities rickshaws are the most common taxi service. In Dhaka alone there are 700,000 rickshaws running each day. Relatively low-cost and nonpolluting cycle rickshaws nevertheless cause traffic congestion and have been banned from many parts of the city.

Trains are also popular. There are nearly 1,720 miles (2,768 km) of railway lines running through Bangladesh. Bangladesh Railway's headquarters are located in the southern port city of Chittagong, which had historically been the southeastern end of the Assam-Bengal Railway. After independence from Pakistan in 1971 only a small length of additional new tracks was laid.

The most common mode of transportation between towns, and indeed the distinguishing feature of Bangladesh's transportation system, is by water, on boats and ferries that operate along the many waterways. A paddle-wheel steamer runs between Dhaka and Khulna regularly, and many other ferries shuttle passengers from port to port.

Bangladesh has international airports at Dhaka, Chittagong, and Sylhet, as well as six domestic airports. Bangladesh Biman Airlines is the state-owned airline.

TOURISM

Tourism in Bangladesh is a slowly developing foreign currency earner. Although news reports of famine, floods, and political unrest have done little to improve foreign perception of Bangladesh, increasing numbers of tourists are attracted to the country's sights and culture. Tourist attractions include historical sites in Dhaka and Chittagong and the beaches of Cox's Bazar, the town founded in 1798 by Captain Hiram Cox of the East India Company.

The best time to visit Bangladesh is from November to February, as the temperatures are between 59°F and 77°F (between 15°C and 25°C) and rainfall is low. Many travelers also use Bangladesh as a link to India, taking advantage of cheap flights from Europe.

TRADE

Bangladesh's chief exports include ready-made garments, jute, fish and shrimp, hides, skins, leather, and tea. Textile yarn and fabrics, machinery and transportation equipment, petroleum, chemicals, iron, steel, cement, and food are some of its major imports.

Its top trading partners include the United States, India, the United Kingdom, Japan, China, Germany, France, Kuwait, and Singapore.

Professor Muhammad Yunus, a professor of economics from the University of Chittagong, first came up with the idea of the Grameen Bank (which literally means "Bank of the Villages" in Bangladesh) in 1976. Yunus was concerned by the extraordinary poverty that surrounded him. Speaking to a poor village woman, he discovered that she earned just a few cents a day weaving, most of which she had to give to the merchant who rented her a loom and to local moneylenders, who charged an outrageous 50 percent interest. Yunus heard many similar stories from villagers and he became determined to find a way to help release these people from the debilitating poverty and debts that ruled their lives.

What came about was a revolutionary banking system that promoted several ideals: to provide banking facilities for the poor; to eliminate the exploitation of moneylenders; to create opportunities for self-employment for the underemployed and unemployed; to raise economic, social, and political awareness among members; and, most importantly, to provide an escape from the cycle of "low income, low savings, low investments, low income" to a cycle of "low income, investment, more income, more investment, more income."

The Grameen Bank's customers are the landless; most of them have never dealt with a lending institution. About 97 percent of the borrowers are women. People require loans for various activities, such as housing, business enterprises, and financial investments. The Grameen Bank provided 200,000 people with collateral-free loans in its first 10 years and had a 98 percent recovery rate of

loans, despite many doubts that poor people, especially women, would be able to honor their debts. In place of the collateral required by conventional banks, small groups of about five people come together to create a morally binding guarantee that the loan will be paid back. "Bicycle bankers" are employed to work in the field, supervising the borrowers' finances. Bicycle bankers, using bicycles or motorcycles, go to a borrower's neighborhood for the weekly meetings. Typically, ten or so groups of five borrowers (60 individual borrowers total) meet every week for about an hour to pay back existing loans, to receive new loans, and to exchange ideas in an open and transparent way in front of the whole group of fellow borrowers.

The Grameen Bank has had astounding success in improving the economic condition of thousands of Bangladeshis. It has had a major impact on poverty alleviation, lifting 58 percent of its clients above the poverty line and providing the means for self-employment beyond agricultural labor. One unusual feature of the Grameen Bank is that it is owned by the poor borrowers of the bank. Of the total equity of the bank, the borrowers own 94 percent, and the remaining 6 percent is owned by the government of Bangladesh. Since its inception, the bank has distributed $6.55 billion (in U.S. dollars) in loans. Out of this, $5.87 billion has been repaid.

ENVIRONMENT

A man fishing on one of Bangladesh's many rivers.

CHAPTER 5

T HE OUTLOOK FOR the environment of Bangladesh is bleak. Aquatic and floodplain ecosystems continue to be severely degraded. The wetland ecosystems have lost connections with larger water bodies (rivers and canals) due to siltation, the process by which a path or channel is gradually choked or obstructed with silt, and land filling or draining for agriculture and homestead use.

More than 50 percent of seasonal and perennial wetlands have been affected by growing unplanned urban and agricultural land use. Upstream water use in Nepal, India, Bhutan, and Tibet greatly reduces dry season water flows into Bangladesh. True forest habitat is less than 6 percent of the total land area and is declining rapidly. Massive deforestation has resulted in loss of biodiversity and productivity of tropical forest resources.

LAND POLLUTION

Poverty with rapid population growth, the absence of a proper land-use policy, and other forces compel people in Bangladesh to exploit natural resources. The quality of the soil has deteriorated due to the use of agrochemicals, encroachment on forest areas for agriculture and settlements, and improper disposal of hazardous industrial

The environment in Bangladesh has been subjected to air, water, and land pollution. A lack of urban planning has also meant that waste and sewage disposal is not well developed, further compounding the problem. Bangladesh's increasing population also puts a strain on the country's resources, and more forests are being cut down to provide wood for fuel.

Littering and disposal of waste materials is also a problem in Bangladesh.

waste materials. In addition, urban sprawl and infrastructure development have reduced the availability of land. Natural events such as cyclones and floods cause land loss as well.

WATER POLLUTION

The environment, economic growth, and development of Bangladesh are all highly influenced by water—its regional and seasonal availability, as well as its quality. Water availability is highly dependent on the monsoon climate and the physical geography of the country. In terms of quality, the surface water of the country is unprotected from untreated industrial waste, materials and municipal wastewater, runoff pollution from chemical fertilizers and pesticides and oil, and lubricant spillage in the coastal area from the operation of sea and river ports and ship breakage. Water quality degrades in the dry season. In particular, water quality around Dhaka is so poor that water from the surrounding rivers can no longer be considered a supply source for human consumption. Among the polluted areas, the worst problems are in the River Buriganga, where the most significant source of pollution appears to be from tanneries in the Hazaribagh area.

ARSENIC CONCENTRATION IN GROUNDWATER

The arsenic concentration in the groundwater is a major problem in Bangladesh today. High levels of arsenic cause serious human health problems if consumed for a long time (from 5 to 15 years). These health issues include skin ailments, damage to internal organs, skin and lung cancer, and eventual death. Recent major studies carried out on arsenic reveal that among 30,000 tubewells—devices installed into a well to abstract groundwater from an aquifer—analyzed, 2,000 exceeded the national standard of 0.05 mg/l for drinking purposes (the World Health Organization [WHO] guideline is 0.01 mg/l). The most seriously affected districts are in and around Chandpur. It has been estimated that more than 20 million people drink water that exceeds the national standard for arsenic levels.

AIR POLLUTION

There are two major sources of air pollution in Bangladesh: vehicular emissions and industrial emissions. Exposure to air pollution is the main environmental threat to human health in many towns and cities. Particulate pollution, also known as PM, is a complex mixture of extremely small particles and liquid droplets. Particle pollution is made up of a number of components, including acids (such as nitrates and sulfates), organic chemicals, metals, and soil or dust particles, on its own, or in combination with sulfur dioxide, leads to ill health, causing at least 500,000 premature deaths, and 4 to 5 million new cases of chronic bronchitis each year. Sulfur dioxide is the chemical compound with the formula SO_2.

The air quality has progressively deteriorated due to the unprecedented growth in the number of passenger vehicles, two-stroke engine vehicles (an internal-combustion engine whose cycle is completed in two strokes of a piston) and continuous industrial and residential development.

The country does have a number of laws and regulations to address air pollution. But there are several additional measures that could be stringently enforced to reduce emissions from vehicles with two-stroke engines, which are the major polluters. Proper inspection and maintenance and the use of low-smoke lubricants could reduce emissions by two-thirds.

NATURAL DISASTERS

Bangladesh is a disaster-prone country. Almost every year one or more severe natural disasters upset people's lives. Flood is a recurring phenomenon, which results in human deaths, loss of livestock, spread of disease and hunger, damaged crops, and destruction of physical and economic infrastructure. Cyclone and storm surges occur frequently and cause significant destruction in the coastal areas of the country. Tropical cyclones and tornadoes have a severe impact on the economy as well as the environment. Although

Deforestation has contributed to loss of forest habitat.

Bangladesh—which has a monsoon climate—usually has enough rain, droughts often hit the northwestern part of the country. Disastrous land erosion takes place along the banks of the major river systems of the country.

CONSERVATION LAWS

Although laws relating to the environmental can be traced to as early as the Penal Code of 1860, it is only during the last decade or so that major environmental law reforms have taken place in Bangladesh. The Bangladesh Environmental Conservation Act of 1995 (ECA) is undoubtedly the flagship legislation in the environmental sector. It deals with the conservation of the environment, improvement of environmental standards, and control and mitigation of environmental pollution. It also provides the definition of the term *pollution*. Coupled with the Environmental Conservation Rules of 1997, the ECA has set a new standard for conservation of the environment. A special court was established by the Environment Court Act of 2000. It now hears cases involving matters related to environment.

DEFORESTATION

Fuelwood is the major wood product used in Bangladesh. Bangladesh needs over 282.5 million cubic feet (8 million cubic meters) of fuelwood every year. Domestic cooking uses an estimated 63 percent, which is 180.1 million cubic feet (5.1 million cubic meters) annually. Industrial and commercial use is also significant, totalling 102.5 million cubic feet (2.9 million cubic meters) annually. Due to limited alternative sources of energy the rural people are mainly dependent on fuelwood for cooking and other household activities.

WASTE TREATMENT AND DISPOSAL

Environment advisor C. S. Karim has made it a requirement that all industries polluting the water and environment by releasing waste must have an Effluent Treatment Plant (ETP) by October 2007 to remove the unwanted hazardous chemicals from the wastewater to meet the statutory pollution control requirements, especially for chemicals, pharmaceuticals, and phosphating and electroplating wastewaters. However, in May 2008, experts commented at a conference that unsupervised industrialization was destroying the country's rivers, and to turn the fatal tide there had to be an effective river protection authority with the power to penalize industries.

A Bangladeshi boy using the outhouse. A lack of proper sewage disposal has contributed to the pollution of the country's rivers.

ENDANGERED ANIMALS

THE GANGES RIVER DOLPHIN The Ganges River dolphin has a long beak, a stocky body, and large flippers. Its eye lacks a lens, and the dolphin is sometimes referred to as being blind, although its eyes do seem to function as a direction-finding device. The Ganges River dolphin measures 4.9 to 8.2 feet (1.5—2.5 m) in length and weighs up to 200 pounds (90 kg). It is found only in fresh water in Bangladesh and India, where the rivers flow slowly through the plains, as well as in Nepal, where the dolphin can be found in relatively clear water and rapids. It is almost certainly declining in number and will continue to do so, as habitat degradation shows no sign of stopping.

THE HISPID HARE The hispid hare is also called the bristly rabbit because it has coarse, dark brown hair. Its ears are short, and its back legs are not much larger than its front legs. It weighs about 4.5 to 5.5 pounds (2—2.5 kg). Its diet consists mainly of bark, shoots, and the roots of grasses, including thatch species, and occasionally crops. The hispid hare was formerly found from Uttar Pradesh in India along the Himalayan foothills, and south to Dhaka in Bangladesh. It has declined due to habitat loss.

The hoolock gibbon is an endangered species.

THE HOOLOCK GIBBON The hoolock gibbon is a small arboreal ape that weighs a little over 13 pounds (6 kg). The adult male is always black, except for its prominent white eyebrows, while the adult female is gold, buff, or brownish-buff. The hoolock gibbon is found in good-quality semi-evergreen/deciduous forest up to 4,500 feet tall (1371.6 m). The hoolock gibbon was formerly widespread from eastern India through Bangladesh to China and south to the Irrawaddy River in Myanmar. Because of threats such as habitat loss and hunting, its numbers have decreased.

FLORA OF BANGLADESH

Each season produces a special variety of flowers in Bangladesh. The prolific water hyacinth is one of them—its carpet of thick green leaves and blue flowers gives the impression that solid ground lies underneath. Other decorative plants, such as jasmine, water lily, rose, hibiscus, bougainvillea, magnolia, and an incredible diversity of wild orchids, are widespread in the forested areas.

NATIONAL PARKS

Protected areas in Bangladesh cover some 2 percent of the country's total area or 602,137 acres (243,677 ha). There are ten national parks, eight wildlife sanctuaries, five ecoparks, one game reserve, and one safari park in Bangladesh.

BHAWAL NATIONAL PARK   Located in Gazipur in the Dhaka Division of Bangladesh, the Bhawal National Park was established in 1974. It covers an area of some 12,410 acres (5,022 ha). This area is home to an incredibly diverse array of flora and fauna. The area was once covered by a lush forest canopy created by Sal trees. Illegal deforestation has stripped the area of much of this natural vegetation—in fact only 148,263 acres (60,000 ha) remain of what was once a magnificent forest. New trees and woodlands have been planted in an effort to help the forest recover, but it will most likely take many years before these trees are mature enough to support the incredible animal diversity that was once so common in this area. Only a few animal species still remain in this small strip of protected vegetation.

KAPTAI NATIONAL PARK   The Kaptai National Park is situated in the Rangamati Hill District, which falls between the Karnaphuly and Kaptai mountain ranges. The area is managed by the Chittagong Hill Tracts Southern Forestry Division and covers an area of some 13,501.8 acres (5,464 ha). It is still a relatively new park, having been established in 1999. Some of the animals that inhabit the park include the elephant, deer, jungle cat, and monkey. A tropical rain forest is found on the banks of the Karnaphuly River. As early as 1873 massive plantations of forest trees were started by local forest management, which has resulted in much of the growth that is seen today. The Kaptai Hydro-Electric Project provides an ecofriendly source of electricity for the people.

HIMCHARI NATIONAL PARK   To protect the area from encroaching developments, Himchari National Park was established in 1980 just south

Bangladesh is party to the following agreements on the environment: Biodiversity, Climate Change, Desertification, Endangered Species, Climate Change-Kyoto Protocol, Environmental Modification, Hazardous Wastes, Law of the Sea, Ozone Layer Protection, Ship Pollution, and Wetlands.

of Cox's Bazar town by the Bangladeshi government as a conservation area for research, education, and recreation. The stomping grounds of herds of Asian elephants, Himchari is still home to these majestic animals. Many of the herbs found in Himchari National Park have therapeutic properties that the local people understand and use.

RAMSAGAR NATIONAL PARK Located in the Dinajpur District in the northwest of Bangladesh, Ramsagar National Park spreads out over an area of about 68.6 acres (27.76 ha), with a vast man-made water reservoir as its focal point. The water reservoir was built between 1750 and 1755 to provide local inhabitants with safe drinking water. Its construction was initiated by Raja Ram Nath, and some 1.5 million laborers worked on the project. The reservoir was named in Nath's honor. The lake is populated by a variety of fish, as well as freshwater crocodiles. The lake is also a stopover for many migratory waterfowl, which makes for a spectacular sight during the migration season.

NIJHUM DWEEP NATIONAL PARK A significant portion of the small island of Nijhum Dweep (also referred to as Nijhum Dwip), located in the Bay of Bengal under the jurisdiction of the Noakhali District of Bangladesh, was designated in 2001 as the Nijhum Dweep National Park. The park is rich in plant and animal species, and is also home to plentiful birdlife, hosting numerous migratory birds. The forestry department of Bangladesh created lush mangrove forests in Nijhum Dweep as part of conservation efforts for the area.

SATCHARI NATIONAL PARK The name *Satchari* means "seven streams," a reference to the streams that flow through the park, providing plentiful water for the lush semi-evergreen forests and other flora, as well as the many animals that live there. Part of the park was at one time planted with eucalyptus and acacia trees, many of which still remain. Satchari National Park is home to the critically endangered hoolock gibbon. Another resident primate is the Phayre's leaf monkey. The village of Tiprapara, which is inhabited by 23 households, lies within the Satchari National Park.

There is great potential in Bangladesh for biodiversity-based sustainable development. In spite of the threatened wild fauna and flora, there are nearly 10,000 species of plants, animals, and microbial organisms—a good percentage of which are found in superabundance.

SHIP BREAKING

Hundreds of ships meet their death every year on the beaches of Bangladesh. The ships are dissected, bolt by bolt, rivet by rivet, with every piece of metal destined to be melted down in furnaces and made into steel rods. Men who work here dissect the ships by hand. The most sophisticated technology on the beach is a blowtorch. The men carry metal plates, each weighing more than a ton, from the shoreline to waiting trucks. Bangladesh desperately needs steel for construction but has no iron-ore mines. The ship-breaking yards are its mines, providing 80 percent of the nation's steel.

But steel is only part of the deal; there are many things on a ship that can be sold off. Ship breaking is a gigantic recycling operation. One can find everything, including kitchen sinks, at a sprawling roadside market that goes on for miles. When you're driving down this road, it's not a problem if you need a toilet or a lifeboat or a light bulb. It is estimated that 97 percent of the ships' contents are recycled. The other 3 percent materials, which are of no commercial value—including the hazardous waste, asbestos, arsenic, and mercury—are left behind to foul the beaches. Environmentalists have been doing battle with the ship-breaking industry for years. They say that the West has no business dumping its toxic waste on impoverished lands in the East. They condemn the appalling work conditions, the low pay, and the lack of accountability for workers who are killed or injured. However, if the ship-breaking industry were to be stopped, it would put 30,000 men out of work and deprive Bangladesh of its source of steel.

It was originally established to accommodate laborers at the cultivated forest plantations.

TEKNAF GAME RESERVE   Located on the banks of the Naf River in the Teknaf Upazila of Cox's Bazar, the Teknaf Game Reserve is one of the five protected areas in Bangladesh where the Forest Department has put into place an approach to ecotourism under the banner of "Nishorgo—Bangladesh's Protected Area Management Program." A highlight of the Teknaf Game Reserve is the Kudum Cave, more commonly referred to as the "Bat Cave," for obvious reasons. Because it is the only known remaining sand-mud cave in Bangladesh, conservationists are keen to preserve it as an ecotourism attraction.

BANGLADESHIS

A Bangladeshi girl carrying a large water pot to collect water.

BANGLADESH IS ONE OF THE TEN most populous countries in the world, with a population about half that of the United States living in an area slightly smaller than Wisconsin. It is also the most densely populated of all countries, having an area of over 1,000 square miles (2,600 square km). Bangladesh's population density is 2,970 people per square mile (1,147 per square km).

Since gaining independence, Bangladesh has experienced massive population growth. In 1996 the country had an estimated population

A Bangladeshi family.

of 153 million and a growth rate of 2.022 percent. Bangladeshi women have a high fertility rate, averaging 3.08 children per woman. This, coupled with a comparatively low ratio of deaths (8 per 1,000) to births (28.86 per 1,000), means a rapidly increasing and young population. One-third of Bangladesh's population is under the age of 15.

Average life expectancy is low, at 63.21 years, compared to over 78 years for developed countries such as the United States, Japan, and the United Kingdom. The individual life expectancy averages for Bangladeshi men and women are similar, despite higher incidences of malnutrition and disease among women.

SOCIAL CLASSES

The Bangladeshi class system is not, in general, rigidly stratified. The social classes are mostly functional and allow considerable mobility. These classes are generally defined by wealth and power as opposed to hereditary social distinctions. In addition, Islam has fairly egalitarian principles that influence social structure.

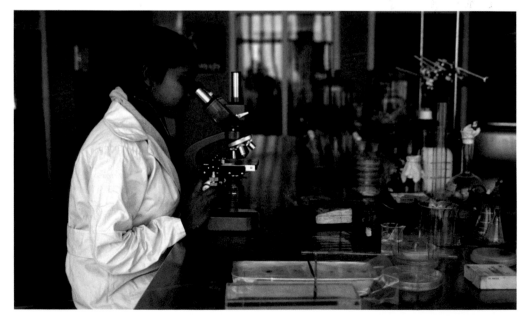

Professionals, like this researcher, are the highest caste of Hindus in Bangladesh.

The caste system traditionally observed by Hindus has not featured very strongly in the Hindu communities of Bangladesh. About 75 percent of Bangladeshi Hindus belong to low-caste and untouchable groups; only a small minority are of the middle or professional caste, and none are high caste. The professionals are therefore the highest caste of Hindus in Bangladesh. However, being Urdu speakers, they became somewhat alienated in independent Bangladesh. In the social arena, the castes are increasingly able to interact with one another. Although all Hindus will identify themselves with a particular caste, caste distinction has gradually come to play a less significant role than it traditionally played in Hindu society.

ATTITUDES

Bangladeshi attitudes are very much rooted in village traditions. Bangladesh is predominantly a country of rural people living simple country lives, and while modern ideas occasionally influence thinking, the attitudes of the people are dominated by traditional beliefs, customs, and manners.

Many rural Bangladeshi still adhere to traditional ways of living.

Bangladeshi women in saris.

DRESS

Bangladeshi men and women dress modestly. Women generally wear saris. The sari, a cloth several yards long, is of a width that stretches from waist to ankle. It is wound around the body from the waist, over an ankle-length slip or blouse, and its free end is thrown over one shoulder. Muslim women drape the free end around their head, and sometimes over the lower part of their face. Cotton saris are worn during the workday, while silk ones are reserved for special occasions. Muslim women, in particular, favor bright colors and patterns and like to decorate their clothes with intricate embroidery. For a wedding, it is traditional for the bride to wear red and yellow.

Men wear a *lungi* (LOONG-gee), a garment similar to the sarong worn by the Malays of Southeast Asia, that is wrapped around the waist. This is usually accompanied by a Western-style shirt. For formal occasions a man may wear an ankle-length, collarless jacket called a *sherwani* (sher-WAH-nee), a turban, and traditional decorative slippers called *nagra* (NAH-grah)

A Chittagong Hill tribe family.

Businesspeople and professionals, especially men, may wear Western-style clothes, including pants, shirt, and tie, as they go about their work in the cities. However, it is still uncommon to find Bangladeshis wearing Western dress elsewhere. Very few Bangladeshi women will be seen wearing pants, short skirts, or revealing dresses in public—doing so would likely result in strong social disapproval.

ETHNIC MINORITIES

JUMMAS *Jumma* is a generic term that refers to the people of 12 distinct tribes living in the Chittagong Hill Tracts. With a population of fewer than a million people, Jummas constitute less than 1 percent of the total population of Bangladesh. They are of Sino-Tibetan descent and have distinct Mongolian features. Essentially an agricultural people, they practice swidden cultivation, locally known as *jhum* ("juhm"), from which their name is derived. Their

The swidden method of cultivation, also called slash-and-burn or shifting cultivation, is practiced by many cultures around the world. In this method the area that is farmed is rotated every few years, so that no area becomes overworked and damaged. At the start of each season, when a new field is needed, an area of several acres is slashed and burned, clearing the area of all vegetation. The ash that falls over the ground serves as a natural fertilizer on top of the thin forest soils. The earth is then prepared and sown by hand.

In the first couple of years the yield is bountiful. However, with exposure to the sun, the thick, moist loam on the forest floor begins to degenerate into barren sand and clay. At this point the farmers will abandon the site and clear a new field. Because the land has not been allowed to degenerate too much, the natural forests soon reclaim the old field and restore the richness in the soil. That patch of land will not be cultivated again for many years, long enough for the natural vegetation to rejuvenate.

chosen style of agriculture makes Jummas relatively nomadic; they do not have permanent homes but move around constantly. Swidden cultivation, also known as shifting cultivation or, more negatively and judgmentally, as "slash and burn agriculture," continues to be a major type of people-forest interaction in Laos, Vietnam, Cambodia, Thailand, and parts of southern China, as well as Indonesia and Papua New Guinea.

The tribes are largely Buddhist and their practices are a combination of Buddhism and tribal religion. Each tribe has a unique language, mostly deriving from the Tibeto-Burmese language family, and a unique system of social organization. In the past there was intertribal warfare, but in recent years, the tribes have formed an alliance based on common land and history, as opposed to religion, language, or culture.

BIHARIS The Biharis are Urdu-speaking, non-Bengali Muslims who originally came from Bihar in northern India as refugees. Before independence the

Bangladesh's national anthem was composed by Rabindranath Tagore (1861—1941), who won the Nobel Prize in literature in 1913.

My Bengal of gold, I love you
Forever your skies, your air set my heart in tune
        as if it were a flute,
In Spring, Oh mother mine, the fragrance from
        your mango-groves makes me wild with joy—
        Ah what a thrill!

In Autumn, Oh mother mine,
        in the full-blossomed paddy fields,
I have seen spread all over—sweet smiles!
Ah, what beauty, what shades, what an affection
        and what a tenderness!
What a quilt have you spread at the feet of
        banyan trees and along the banks of rivers!
Oh mother mine, words from your lips are like
        nectar to my ears!
        Ah, what a thrill!
If sadness, Oh mother mine, casts a gloom on your face,
        my eyes are filled with tears!

Biharis were the dominant people of Bengali society. As a result, they did not stand to benefit from the separation from Pakistan.

During the war they chose to ally themselves with Pakistan. When independence was announced for Bangladesh, hundreds of thousands of Biharis were repatriated to Pakistan, leaving only 600,000 Biharis in Bangladesh.

LIFESTYLE

Men transporting goods.

BANGLADESH IS ONE OF the least urbanized countries in the world. About 80 percent of its population lives in the country, and village life, with agriculture providing work, is the typical lifestyle for most Bangladeshis.

Nevertheless, as in the rest of the developing world, Bangladesh's cities have become beacons attracting those who seek a better life for themselves and their families. Young males form the majority of those who make the journey to the urban centers to find work in the new industries that accompany development. In manufacturing, for example, male workers outnumber female workers almost three to one.

Two women weaving straw baskets. Many of these women are uneducated and make a living out of selling their wares.

The majority of Bangladeshis are engaged in agriculture and live and work in rural areas. Increasingly more young males are leaving their rural homes and moving to urban areas and even overseas in search of jobs. Women are expected to remain at home to tend to the family and household. Many marriages are still arranged and dowries, although illegal, are still paid.

The more adventurous seek work in the more dynamic economies of Asia, with many heading for the plantations, construction sites, and service industries of countries such as Malaysia and Singapore.

SOCIAL CONVENTIONS

GREETINGS Bangladeshis greet one another by saying "*Shagatom*" (SHAH-gah-tom), which means "welcome." Some people also say "*Salaam aleykum*" (Sah-LAAM ah-lee-KUM), meaning "peace be unto you." The standard greeting among Bangladeshi Hindus is *namoshkar* (Na-mosh-KAAR), where the head is bowed and the palms are placed together in front of the chest with fingers pointing upward, as if praying.

GENDER SEPARATION There is very strict gender separation within the Muslim community. In school, boys and girls are seated separately, and

A group of boys at an Islamic school. Girls and boys are usually separated.

It is assumed that there are around 350,000 Bangladeshi workers in Malaysia. Workers range from unskilled working in manufacturing, construction, and plantation to highly skilled ones, including top engineers who have worked to construct Petronas towers, an icon of Malaysia's miraculous development. Estimates show that these workers spend around 80 percent of their income in Malaysia, contributing to and revitalizing the local economy.

NO OFFENSE INTENDED!

There are a number of body gestures that Westerners use at home that would be interpreted as grave insults by a Bangladeshi. The act of raising your thumb to someone, for example, is a friendly gesture of encouragement or approval in the United States. In Bangladesh, however, this is considered very rude.

It is acceptable for men to sit cross-legged and for women to sit with their legs tucked beneath them and to one side on the floor or cushions, but it is taboo to display the soles of your feet. It is also offensive to offer money as a gift.

Men and women are expected to dress and behave modestly. Flirting is considered to be completely unacceptable.

they are also given different areas to play. Within the home certain areas are designated specifically as "male" or "female" areas. Women and men are segregated in the mosque when they go to pray, and there are certain places that women will rarely go, such as a bank.

BIRTH

Many Bangladeshi women, particularly in the rural areas, give birth at home rather than in a hospital. The women often go to their natal home, especially to have their first child. A room in the house is designated for this purpose and is called the *atur ghar* (ah-TOO ghor), or birthing room, for 40 days after the birth. The baby is born in the presence of female relatives or friends. If a midwife is called in—rarely in the case of poor families—she will often only come to cut the umbilical cord. Poor women must deliver the baby themselves.

Childbirth is regarded as highly polluting to both the mother and her surroundings. After childbirth the mother and the newborn are confined to the birthing room for up to nine days, and allowed out only for natural functions. Even then the mother must be accompanied by another woman, and must carry a sickle and a burning dung stick to protect her from evil spirits, to which she is believed to be vulnerable at this time.

Bangladeshi men will shake the hand of a Western man, but when introduced to a woman they simply nod their heads, as it is taboo for a man to touch a woman who is not a family member.

Bangladesh has a high birthrate.

A small fire burns constantly in the birthing room. Filling the room with smoke is said to protect the mother and baby from harmful spirits. After her confinement is over the mother has a ritual bath, the birthing room is swept and plastered, and the bed linen is boiled to purify it. Forty days after the birth the mother and the birthing room are ritually cleansed again, and then the mother resumes her usual activities.

MARRIAGE

Marriages are usually arranged by the bride's father or another male guardian. Either the proposed bride or groom may refuse a match; however, this is rare, as it is a social disgrace to do so. Although girls traditionally marry at the onset of puberty, the average age has increased in recent years to around 18. There is usually a considerable age difference between the bride and the groom. Dowries are traditional and, despite laws prohibiting the practice, are still usually offered and accepted. It was found that the rate of early marriage dropped from about 50 percent in 2004 to 42 percent in 2006 as Bangladeshi women's educational levels are slowly going up.

Wedding ceremonies vary depending on the religion of the bride and groom. Muslim-style weddings are most common, although most weddings incorporate cultural elements into the religious traditions. There are usually four parts to a Bangladeshi wedding: the *gae halud* (gay ho-LUTH), *akht* (AHKT), the *mala badol* (MAY-lah BA-dol), and the *bou bhat* (boa BAHT).

The *gae halud* translates as the "turmeric ceremony" and originates from a Bengali tradition. One ceremony is held for the bride and another for the groom, with the bride's generally taking place first. Friends and family of the groom arrive with gifts of saris, jewelry, and cosmetics for the bride, and the bride's family gives them sweets and flower petals. The bride sits on a dais decorated with flowers and the groom's mother ties a golden-fringed bracelet around her wrist as a symbol of betrothal. Well-wishers then approach the dais one by one to place a bit of turmeric on the bride's face and their own, and then feed the bride something sweet. The groom's ceremony is similar.

Family members examine the wedding finery of the bride.

The *akht* ceremony, which is part of Islamic tradition, is the legal declaration of marriage. As in a Christian wedding, the bride and groom exchange vows. First the consent of the groom is obtained without the bride present, and then the groom asks the bride if she consents. She accepts by saying *kobul* (koh-BUL, meaning "I accept") three times. The couple then share the fruit of a date palm, an Islamic custom.

The *mala badol* is a ceremony in which the bride and groom exchange garlands, symbolizing their union. A muslin cloth is placed over the head of the couple and they share a spicy yogurt drink. Then they glance at one another through a mirror. Traditionally this glance was the first time that the bride and groom would have seen one another.

Several days later the groom's family hosts the *bou bhat* ("bride's rice"), which is a reception for the newlyweds. This is the first time that the couple steps out socially as husband and wife.

DEATH

It is Islamic custom to prepare the deceased by washing the body and wrapping it in a shroud. The body is then buried and the men pray.

Women do not participate in the burial or burial prayers, nor do they visit graves because their presence is believed to contaminate the sacred ground.

Mandi (an ethnic minority) villagers attending a funeral.

RURAL LIFE

About 80 percent of Bangladeshis live in the country, reflecting the high proportion of agricultural workers. The rural Bangladeshi home, or *bari* (BAH-ree), typically consists of a collection of individual huts gathered around a central courtyard. The plot of land is usually rectangular, with the narrow end abutting the street. The different areas of a *bari* have specific purposes. On the street side of the house is a fairly large area called the *goli* (GOH-lee). This is a semiprivate space that is mainly used by men for socializing and receiving male guests.

The *ghar* are the individual one- or two-room huts. They are generally constructed with mud walls and thatched roofs, and often have no windows and only one doorway for light. They are used mostly for storage and sleeping, although work moves inside during wet weather. The *ghar* are focused around the courtyard, which is the most important part of the *bari*. This is where all the daily activities, socializing, and celebrations take place.

A farmer with his cattle in the village of Hoaikong.

Cooking and the kitchen are considered to be a woman's domain.

The courtyard is the women's area, and while nonrelated females may move freely through the courtyards of neighbors, the courtyard is kept private from unrelated males. For a man to enter the courtyard uninvited is perceived as a symbolic violation. The *kanta* (KAN-tah) is the garden at the rear of the *bari*. It contains the vegetable patch, bamboo grove, and fruit trees, and often a private pond for bathing. There is also a handpump for drawing water. The *kanta* is also a woman's domain.

A *bari* is typically inhabited by an extended family, with each nuclear family having its own *ghar*, but all sharing the other areas of the *bari*. Sons will build their own *ghar* when they marry, but will remain under their father's authority, and their wives under their mother-in-law's guidance. When the father dies, sons will often start their own separate households.

URBAN LIFE

Approximately 20 percent of Bangladeshis live in an urban environment. Towns are populated mostly by government employees, merchants, and

A BANGLADESHI HOUSEWARMING

When a new house is built, a traditional Bangladeshi buries a nail under each of its four corners in the belief that this keeps it from falling down. Before moving in, Muslim families will call in a mullah (a learned man) to recite verses from the Koran, the holy book of Islam. Wealthier families may hold a milad *(MI-lahd), a religious gathering to pray and discuss the life of the Prophet Muhammad.*

business operators. Most of these people live in shabby, ramshackle constructions that lack modern amenities. Unlike rural homesteads, urban dwellings are usually shared by a nuclear family. Only occasionally does the extended family live together.

Dhaka and much of urban Bangladesh suffer from poverty and inadequate housing. A quarter of Dhaka's population lives in slums and only 53 percent of Bangladesh's population has access to safe sanitation. However, the average income of the urban poor living in Dhaka slums is three times higher than that of the rural poor. Projections suggest that more than 50 percent of Bangladeshi population will be living in urban areas of Bangladesh by the year 2025. This acceleration of urbanization presents huge challenges for the government.

Slum dwellers in Dhaka. Despite their poor living conditions they still earn more than the rural poor.

WOMEN'S ROLES

Muslim countries are overwhelmingly male-dominated. Being allowed to walk out of the front door is something that women in most countries around the world take for granted. For many women in Bangladesh this right has to be won through struggle, as along with other rights such as not being

Young children in school. There has been an increase in the number of girls attending school.

married off as a child, being able to have economic independence, having protection from illegal divorce, and the practice of dowry.

Traditionally there is a strict division of labor according to gender: Men are the income earners, and women perform work in the household. A woman's duties include hand-grinding flour and spices, taking care of animals other than cattle (this being the man's job), tending the vegetable garden, pumping water, replastering, repairing the home when necessary, and processing and storing farm produce. Employment opportunities have been more available for women than for men in the last decade, with the growth of the export garment industry in Dhaka and Chittagong. Almost 80 percent of the 1.4 million garment sector workers are women. About 43 percent of women work in the agriculture, fisheries, and livestock sectors, but 70 percent of them are unpaid family workers.

EDUCATION

The government of Bangladesh made primary education compulsory for all children between the ages of 6 and 10. This has had a major impact on the system and the gross enrollment rate increased from 75 percent to 95 percent by 1996. Bangladesh has 18 million children in 62,000 primary schools; this is one of the largest primary systems in the world. Over 65 percent of the primary schools are government primary schools, and the rest are registered nongovernmental schools that are still assisted by the government. The government of Bangladesh gives free books and education kits to the students of primary schools. Bangladesh has 7.4 million students enrolled in secondary school. In recent years female school enrollment has improved. Approximately 50 percent of primary and secondary school students are female. Bangladesh has slowly improved its literacy rate to 43.1 percent. However, there is still a big difference between men and women—53 percent of men are literate, compared to only 35 percent for women.

HEALTH

Bangladesh suffers from major health problems. Malnutrition and poor sanitation cause hundreds of deaths every year. Susceptibility to disease is high and availability of treatment low. Although Bangladesh has a basic health-care system in place, it is grossly inadequate in terms of remedies.

A nurse caring for an elderly man in the hospital.

The Bangladeshi government's objective is to provide minimum health-care services for all. In 1996 about 20 million children were inoculated against polio as part of a campaign to wipe out the disease. Down from hundreds of cases in previous years, the number of laboratory-confirmed polio cases declined to 29 in 1999, one in 2000, and none in 2001 and 2002. However, polio reappeared in 2005 and a major inoculation campaign has been reinstituted, and, by late 2008, more than 22 million children had been inoculated against polio. Nevertheless financial constraints and the lack of supplies and personnel continue to inhibit the government's plans. With about 2,571 for every hospital bed, Bangladesh ranks alongside Afghanistan, Ethiopia, and Nepal as one of the countries with the world's lowest number of hospital beds. In contrast, Monaco has 196 hospital beds for every 10,000 people.

RELIGION

Men praying in the mosque.

>BANGLADESH WAS CREATED AS A Muslim country. Some 83 percent of its population is Muslim, making it one of the largest concentrations of Muslims in the world. Hindus form another 16 percent of the population, while Buddhists, Christians, and followers of tribal religions make up the remaining 1 percent.

PRE-ISLAMIC RELIGIONS

Bangladesh's places of worship recall its Buddhist and Hindu heritage. There are still several Buddhist monasteries dating from the seventh

Hindu temples.

Bangladesh is a predominantly Muslim country. The teachings of the Prophet Muhammad influence every aspect of a Muslim's life, including what they eat, what they wear and how they behave. Ideally Muslims pray five times a day. The constitution of Bangladesh allows for the freedom of worship, and the presence of other places of worship bears testament to this.

to ninth centuries A.D., which are protected by the government. Many other monasteries, however, were destroyed by invading Muslim armies in the 13th century, in the belief that they were military fortresses.

THE STORY OF ISLAM

Islam came into existence in A.D. 610, when a man named Muhammad first preached a series of divine revelations to the people of the Arabian city of Mecca. His words were believed to have been told to him by the angel Gabriel, and he was accepted by many as the Prophet of God. Muhammad was a firm monotheist (believer in one God). He became unpopular with many Meccans, and in A.D. 622 he and the followers of his preachings were driven from Mecca to Medina.

This migration marks the beginning of the Muslim calendar. Today Mecca is Islam's holiest city. It is every Muslim's goal to visit Mecca and the Kaaba,

The oldest copy of the Koran in Bangladesh.

a building covered in black cloth that stands in the courtyard of the Great Mosque, the holiest place in Mecca.

Muhammad continued to preach, and after his death in A.D. 632 his divinely inspired speeches were compiled into the Koran, the scripture of Islam. The Koran and the Hadith, a collection of Muhammad's sayings and examples of his personal behavior, are now the comprehensive guides to spiritual, ethical, and social living for millions of Muslims all over the world.

THE FIVE PILLARS OF ISLAM

These are the duties of all Muslims:

SHAHADAH (shah-HAH-dah)   This is a testimonial prayer that states the central belief of Islam—there is no god but Allah, and Muhammad is his Prophet.

SALAT (sah-LAHT) This is a daily prayer recited five times: at sunrise, midday, afternoon, sunset, and evening.

Muslim men prepare to pray. Ideally Muslims should pray five times a day.

Muslim girls dress with modesty in mind. This prepares them for the restrictions of purdah practices, a regulating code of behavior for women. A woman usually drapes the end of her sari over her head when she is in the presence of adult males. Outside her home she often clenches part of her sari with her teeth to hide her face.

ZAKAT (zah-KAHT) *Zakat*, or almsgiving, requires that Muslims give money to the poor or to charitable causes.

SAWM (soom) This is the fast during Ramadan, the ninth month of the Islamic year, when Muslims abstain from various activities, including eating and drinking, between the hours of sunrise and sunset.

HAJJ (hahj) This is the pilgrimage to Mecca. All Muslims should make the pilgrimage to the holy city at least once in their life if they can. Some perform

PRAYER RITUAL

Praying is a very public event in Bangladesh. Whenever possible, men will gather at a mosque. Women sometimes congregate separately from the men, but more often they pray in their homes. The form of prayer is strictly prescribed in Islam. Everybody stands upright, facing toward Mecca, and then performs the following ritual, called rak'a (RAH-kah), which is repeated several times:

- Open the hands.
- Touch the earlobes with the thumbs.
- Lower the hands and fold them, right hand over left.
- Bow from the hips with hands on knees.
- Straighten the body.
- Sink gently to the knees.
- Touch the ground with hands, nose, and forehead, remaining in this position for 10 to 15 seconds.
- Raise the body while kneeling, sitting on the heels.
- Count on the fingers.
- Press the hands, nose, and forehead to the ground again.
- Stand.

Islam has 1.61 billion followers around the world. Some 10.7 million Muslims live in the United States alone. Pakistan, with some 95 percent of its 172,800,048 people professing the religion of Islam, has the world's largest Muslim population.

the hajj many times. A male pilgrim wears a seamless white garment and abstains from sexual relations, shaving, and cutting the hair or nails. While in Mecca the pilgrim performs certain rituals that emulate the actions of figures from Arabic history, such as running between the hills of Safa and Marwa in imitation of Hagar, the wife of Abraham, who was the father of the Arabs. A highlight of the hajj is kissing the sacred black stone of Islam housed in the Kaaba.

HINDUISM

Hindus first overthrew Buddhist rule in the region of Bangladesh in about A.D. 1100, only a century before the Muslim invasion. Hinduism has been a minority religion there ever since. Most religious observances take place in the home, where there is usually a shrine or altar. When Hindus visit a

Hindu Bangladeshis. Freedom of worship is guaranteed in the country's constitution.

temple, it is not generally a community gathering, as with Islamic prayers and Christian services. Instead they go alone or in small groups to pray and worship the gods. Cows are revered by Hindus and are never eaten. Although vegetarianism is common among high-caste Hindus of other countries, most Bangladeshi Hindus of higher caste eat some fish.

BUDDHISM

Buddhism was the dominant religion in Bangladesh before the Muslim conquest. The centers of learning, Buddhism diminished rapidly after invasion of Muslim armies that destroyed the monasteries.

Today there are few Buddhists in Bangladesh. Most are concentrated in the Chittagong Hill Tracts, where there are still several monasteries. Most Buddhist villages have a school where boys live for a time and learn to read Burmese and scriptures in Pali, an Indo-Aryan language. It is not uncommon for adult men to return regularly to their school for periods of retreat.

CHRISTIANITY

Members of the small Christian community of Bangladesh are mostly Roman Catholics. The first Christian settlements were established in Dhaka by the Portuguese in the 17th century. Later Protestant and Baptist missions were also established. The church found a large number of converts, particularly among low-caste Hindus.

LANGUAGE

Signboards written in the national
language of Bangladesh—Bengali.

B ANGLA (ALSO KNOWN AS BENGALI), is the official language of Bangladesh, and is the fifth-most widely spoken language with 211 million native speakers worldwide. There are also several hundred thousand Urdu speakers in Bangladesh, and a number of languages similar to Burmese.

Bangladeshis are generally articulate and expressive, despite their low literacy rate. And more so than in many countries, language in Bangladesh has particular significance in the hearts and minds of its speakers. After having fought a long and gruesome war for the right to speak Bengali, the Bangladeshis now regard their language as a symbol of their nationalism.

DEVELOPMENT OF BENGALI

Bangla/Bengali developed from the Indo-Aryan, part of the Indo-Iranian, branch of the Indo-European language family. It is derived from Prakrit (Middle Indo-Aryan), which was itself derived from Sanskrit. Bangla is identifiable from about A.D. 1000. Buddhist texts found in Nepal, dated between 900 and 1,000 years old, are the oldest known written records in Bangla.

Right: Bangladeshi children in school have the opportunity to learn to read and write in Bengali.

Transactions in shops in Bangladesh are conducted in the language of commerce, Bengali.

The written form has been subjected to remarkably little local variation. The records that exist reveal nearly identical forms of language from divergent civilizations. The spoken language, however, has been gradually conditioned by the various linguistic and ethnic influences in the different regions, and many new Indo-Aryan speech forms have emerged.

Bangla/Bengali developed as a "people's" language and remains so today. One of the earliest records of Bengali is the Buddhist *Charyapad* (CHAH-ree-AH-pad), which was influenced by the ballads and experiences of Buddhist monks of north Bengal who worked among villagers. These writings were themselves influenced by the vernacular of the villagers, and so the language, from its earliest roots, has been a true expression of its speakers, not intellectualized.

FORMAL AND COLLOQUIAL STYLES

Two main styles of Bengali are used. *Sadhubhasa* (SAH-DOO-bah-sah) is the "elegant language." It is the traditional literary style based on the middle

Bengali of the 16th century. The "current language," Chaltibhasa (CHAHL-tee-bah-sah), only really developed during the 20th century. It is based on the cultivated speech of the educated people from around Calcutta.

The differences between the two styles are subtle. The vocabulary is much the same, although there are differences in the forms of pronouns and verbs. Chaltibhasa also uses more colloquialisms, phrases, and idioms than does Sadhubhasa, which uses spoken forms from the formal Sanskrit and Islamic literary traditions.

Many linguists believe that the use of traditional Sanskrit words is a defining characteristic of Sadhubhasa. Because Sanskrit was the language of the elite for centuries, it stands to reason that the academic language of Bengal should be influenced by it.

Other linguists believe the influence is predominantly Persio-Arabic, which is evident in the borrowing of Persio-Arabic words, the re-creation of Islamic ideas, and the use of similes and metaphors in Bengali.

Rural women learning how to read.

Chaltibhasa first became commonly used during the early years of World War I. Today it has almost entirely replaced Sadhubhasa in common speech. Nevertheless Sadhubhasa is still taught in schools as the traditional style. There are also stylistic differences between the different social classes of Chaltibhasa speakers—just as in the English language of Great Britain there are regional and socioeconomic variations in grammar, vocabulary, and pronunciation.

There are distinct variations, for example, between the Bengali spoken by an educated person from Dhaka and that of a factory worker from Khulna. However, they can still understand one another. The distinction between Sadhubhasa and Chaltibhasa can best be compared to the distinction between Shakespearean, aristocratic, and working-class forms of English in Great Britain.

Signs written in Bengali.

Movie and election posters on a wall vie for attention.

THE SCRIPT

Bangla/Bengali, like most scripts of Southern Asia, is derived from the ancient Brahmi alphabet and is related to the *devanagari* script commonly used for Sanskrit. These scripts are midway between alphabets and syllabaries, and consist of symbols that represent a consonant and a vowel sound. Some vowel sounds are written as separate symbols, and these are attached somewhere on the consonant, sometimes even before or after it.

Indian scripts have a unique feature called a "consonant conjunct." This is a process where two consonants that occur together, without an intervening vowel, are conjoined into a single special letter.

THE MEDIA

Bangladesh has more than 1,000 newspapers and magazines, including more than 100 daily newspapers. Major Bengali newspapers include *Dainik*

Jugantor (with a circulation of about 270,000), *Prothom Alo* (223,465), *Dainik Ittefaq* (215,900), and *Dainik Inquilab* (180,140) all published in Dhaka.

The other cities also have their own newspapers, such as *Dainik Azadi* (Chittagong, 20,000) and *Dainik Purbanchal* (Khulna, 5,000). Bangladesh's low literacy rate, however, means that many Bangladeshis do not read these newspapers.

Bangladesh also has a number of English language dailies. These include the *Bangladesh Observer* (circulation: 43,000), *The Bangladesh Times* (27,500), and *The Daily Star* (28,115), all published in Dhaka, and the Khulna-based *Daily Tribune* (5,816). A legacy of decades of British colonial rule, English is widely spoken in urban areas, and many shops and business offices have signs in both Bengali and English. English is also used for some government and legal matters.

Bangladesh has newspapers in English and Bengali, but they are not widely read due to the country's low literacy rate.

Radio Bangladesh and Bangladesh Television were both established in 1971. These organizations merged in 1984 to form the government-controlled National Broadcasting Authority. Radio Bangladesh transmits throughout Bangladesh through its regional stations in Dhaka, Chittagong, Khulna, Rajshahi, Rangpur, and Sylhet. It also transmits to South Asia, the Middle East, Africa, and Western Europe in Bengali, English, Arabic, Hindi, Nepalese, and Urdu via its shortwave station in Dhaka.

Bangladesh Television, which started color transmission in 1980, provides two channels that are available all over the country. However, there are only 5.9 television sets for every 1,000 people, so it is a relatively underutilized medium for communication.

Two men listening to the radio for updates about an ongoing cricket match.

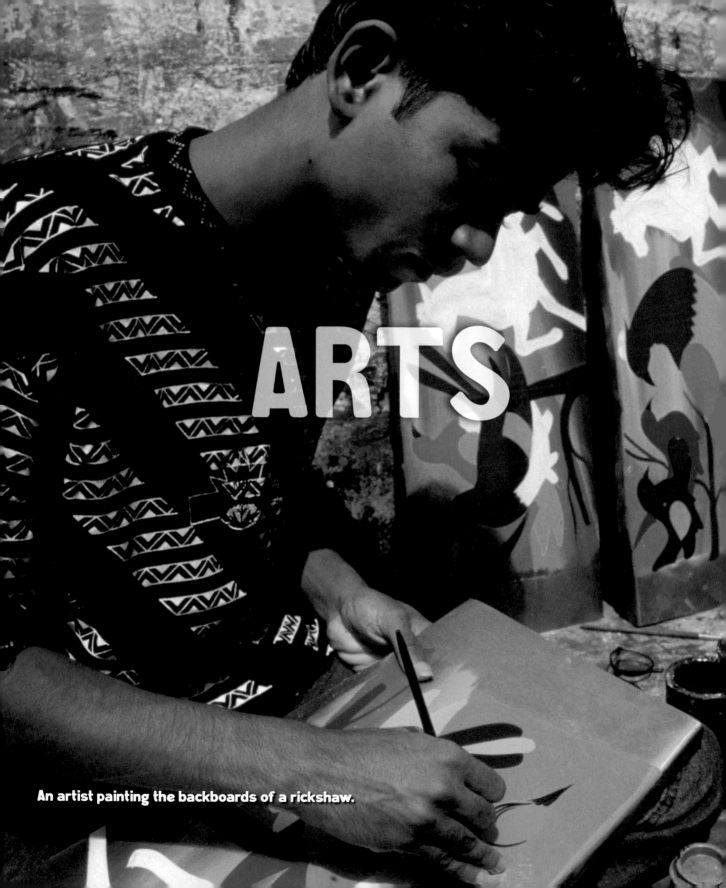

ARTS

An artist painting the backboards of a rickshaw.

ALTHOUGH BANGLADESH HAS A rich tradition in the arts, going as far back as the first millennium A.D., the country's harsh weather has destroyed many ancient pre-Islamic artworks. Nevertheless a few temples and religious monuments that display the traditions of these cultures still stand today.

They provide compelling evidence that a rich and continuous tradition in bronze sculpture, mostly depicting Buddhist and Hindu deities, once thrived here. Stone sculptures dating as early as the second century

A clay mold of a Hindu figurine. Bangladesh has a rich art tradition, particularly in sculptures of Buddhist and Hindu gods.

Bangladesh has a rich artistic tradition, which has continued to today. The influence of Buddhism and Hinduism is inescapable as many artists and sculptors choose to depict deities from these faiths. Art can also be seen everyday in the country's rickshaws, which are all brightly painted and decorated.

Hindu artists painting statues.

A.D., believed to have been decorations in temples or other large buildings, have also been found. The relatively large number of Buddhist sculptures discovered reflects the former dominance of Buddhism in Bangladesh. After the 12th century, production of such sculptures declined sharply, corresponding with the Muslim invasion from the north.

ISLAMIC ART

Islam prohibits Muslim artists from representing human figures in artwork, based on the doctrine that only Allah may create life. Instead Islamic art is characterized by ornate calligraphy and arabesque designs. Passages of the Koran are written elaborately and colorfully decorated with intertwining leaves and flowing patterns.

CONTEMPORARY ART

The works of modern Bangladeshi artists reflect recent trends on the international art scene. Abstract and representative works are produced

NO ORDINARY CANVAS

The streets of Dhaka are filled with some 700,000 rickshaws, which are the principal means of transportation for most Dhakans. Since the 1930s rickshaws have symbolized the daily life of Bangladeshis. In the 1970s Bangladeshi artists began to use rickshaws as a way to display their work.

This trend became so popular that today the painted rickshaw is a cultural phenomenon. Rickshaw owners commission artists to paint vivid, colorful murals all over the rickshaw, including the hood, backseats, and wheels.

Islamic architecture in a Chittagong mosque.

in sculpture, tapestry, engraving, and painting. Several Bangladeshi artists have gained international recognition for their work, including Zainul Abedin, noted for his sketches of the 1943 Bengali famine.

ARCHITECTURE

The evolution of Bangladeshi architecture reflects the attitudes of the ruling powers of the time. For example, the Hindu and Buddhist temples of the pre-Islamic Indian era followed their respective traditional styles. The distinctive arches and domes that have long been recognized as fundamental characteristics of mosques were introduced at the time of the Mogul invasion. Sometimes the styles crossed over, so that Hindu temples were influenced by Islamic architecture, and integrated Islamic features with traditional Hindu elements, such as the terracotta decorations.

European styles of architecture first appeared in churches in Dhaka in and around the 1800s, and a unique hybrid of Mogul and European designs gradually developed. Since the 1960s Bangladesh has felt a really strong Western influence. Most present-day houses are built simply out of wood and bamboo or mud-brick and thatch. Modern commercial architecture is similar to Western styles.

PERFORMING ARTS

The performing arts of Bangladesh, despite recent developments in theater, movies, television, and radio, remain very much centered in the village folk culture. Outdoor stagings of drama, music, and poetry recitations are often seen in the villages, where the arts are most alive and vibrant. This is the principal way that the traditions are continued.

DANCE

Dance forms are almost entirely from Hindu or tribal traditions because dance is not used as a mode of artistic expression in Islam. Hindu dance was originally a prayer, and is still used as such. The classical dance that is popular in Bangladesh today is a combination of Western ballet forms and Hindu styles.

Folk dances take various forms, but the seasons and events of rural life are themes in almost all of them. For example, a dance called *moni puri* (MOH-nee POO-ree) is a celebration by the entire community that takes place on the first full moon night after the harvest. The dances of the Chittagong Hill tribes show distinct influences from neighboring Burma.

Bangladeshi dancers during the Boshonto Utshob festival.

The kirtan *(KEER-tahn) is a Hindu prayer dance. Arms are raised above the head or hands are held together in a prayer position. The way in which the dancer moves and touches the ground with his or her feet is believed to stimulate the chakras, or the centers of energy in the body.*

At the same time, the dancer chants and sings often Sanskrit phrases that praise the gods. The chants, such as "Hare Krishna" and "Babanam Kevalam," are all essentially different ways of expressing the idea of eternal love. The resonance produced in the voice through chanting is said to inspire the same physical feeling that is achieved through meditation.

MUSIC

Bangladeshi music consists of three main categories: the traditional, classical music of the Indian style; folk music; and a modern style influenced by contemporary Western "pop" music. The main melody is usually carried by vocal expression and is supported by instruments.

Sitars (classical Indian stringed instruments), violins, and flutes are favored instruments. Bamboo flutes are especially popular in rural areas, where the haunting songs of herdsmen and boatmen are loved. *Baia* (BY-ah) and tabla drums are used in concerts and for classical music and the *dhole* (DOL), or country drum, is a common village instrument.

Western-style popular music began to influence Bangladeshi music strongly in the early 1970s. Several recording studios were established in Dhaka, which produced many folk and tribal songs and also thousands of pop-style songs about national heroes and martyrs that were written after independence.

DRAMA

Bangladeshis produced little drama prior to the independence movement against the British. With the rise of nationalism in the 1930s, both Muslims

The esraj (EHZ-rahj) is a traditional Bengali instrument. It has a short, waisted chamber—the lower resonance chamber is hollowed out and covered with parchment and a decorated strip of leather at the waist—and a long, broad neck. The player places the base in his or her lap, holding it vertically with the neck resting on his or her left shoulder. The four strings are played with a bow and by pressing along the frets, similar to playing the violin. The soft, mellow tone of the esraj is similar to that of the sarangi (a bowed, short-neck lute). It can be hauntingly beautiful, whether played solo or in a group, or as an accompaniment to vocal music.

and Hindus began to write plays, mainly on the theme of nationalism. Nevertheless there was little in the way of dramatic productions until after 1971, when several companies began to present plays in Dhaka and amateur groups sprang up in Chittagong.

Dramatic performances have, however, never attracted as wide a following as movies. The exceptions are the village folk plays. These *jatra* (JA-trah) plays are by far the most distinctive form of Bangladeshi drama, preserving folk tales in comedy, tragedy, and melodrama.

They are usually outdoor productions, complete with sets, costumes, and makeup, and performed by local actors, singers, dancers, and musicians. Another popular dramatic activity is the *kabiagn* (KA-byne), a poetry contest in which two people debate in impromptu verse. Each contestant is accompanied by a few musical instruments and a vocal chorus that repeats the contestant's lines.

FOLK CRAFT

POTTERY With some 680 villages devoted entirely to the manufacture of pots, pottery is the most common art form in Bangladesh. The pots are made on wheels and in molds by both men and women.

TEXTILES Bengali textiles have for centuries been regarded as being of superior quality. Before British rule, fine muslin was made in the Dhaka region

Two women weaving a red and gold cloth.

and exported as far as Europe. According to folklore, the muslin was so fine and transparent that it took seven layers to conceal the body, and 11 yards (10 m) could be wadded in one hand. It was said that a sari of Dhaka muslin could be drawn through a small finger-ring.

Despite intentional British discouragement of the art, the export of finished textiles to Britain instead encouraged the spread of British-made goods in the colonies, and a high level of skill in weaving has persisted throughout the years, both at the textile mills and at individual looms. Bangladeshi cotton and silk saris are prized all over the subcontinent for the exquisite quality of the fabric, the colorful and intricate, often kaleidoscopic, floral, and geometric designs, and the delicate embroidery.

LITERATURE

At heart, all Bangladeshis are poets.

—Anonymous

I, the eternal rebel,

Shall rest in quiet

only when I find

The sky and the air

free

Of the piteous

groans of the

oppressed.

—Kazi Nazrul Islam

THE BLANK AGE No written records of Bengali literature exist from the period A.D. 1200—1350, and so this time is often referred to as the Blank or Dark Age.

MEDIEVAL LITERATURE A notable feature of medieval Bengali literature is that it was entirely verse. It is mostly centered on religious themes and lyrical poems. Long eulogistic poems—sometimes consisting of tens of thousands

Books for sale at a bookshop.

of lines—appear throughout the period. Not all had religious themes, though. A large number of poems focused on rural life and politics.

MODERN LITERATURE   The British colonization of the Indian subcontinent greatly influenced Bengali literature. European styles of education, Christianity, and the introduction of the English language all played a vital role in shaping the Bengali literary style.

In the late 1800s several events sparked a wave of literary production. First the Bengali script, which had been slowly evolving, developed into the form that exists today, giving Bengali writers a truly Bengali tool to use. Second Bengali nationalism emerged. These two factors led to a cultural renaissance, in which Bengali identity became the main theme. The well-known poet Rabindranath Tagore, who won a Nobel Prize in literature, chose to write all his works in Bengali, even after studying in England for several years.

Rabindranath Tagore's father, Debendranath Tagore (1817–1905), was a noted Hindu philosopher and a religious reformer. Like his son he wrote and published many books in Bengali. His *Brahmo-Dharma* (*The Religion of God*), a commentary on the Sanskrit scriptures published in 1869, is considered a masterpiece by scholars.

Many poems written by Bengali poets are based on the themes of nationalism, independence, and lamented war heroes. Below are two poems by the two most famous Bengali writers, Rabindranath Tagore and Kazi Nazrul Islam.

Tagore achieved international fame for his 1,000 poems, two dozen plays, eight novels, eight volumes of short stories, 2,000 songs (for which he composed the music as well as the lyrics), paintings, lectures, and a mass of prose on literary, religious, social, and political topics. Islam earned the popular nickname "Rebel Poet" for his outspoken, patriotic writings, which were enormously influential in the liberation struggle.

Where the Mind Is Without Fear

Where the mind is without fear and the head is held high
Where knowledge is free
Where the world has not been broken up into fragments
By narrow domestic walls
Where words come out from the depth of truth
Where tireless striving stretches its arms towards perfection
Where the clear stream of reason has not lost its way
Into the dreary desert sand of dead habit
Where the mind is led forward by thee
Into ever-widening thought and action
Into that heaven of freedom, my Father, let my country awake.

—Rabindranath Tagore

Thieves and Robbers

Who calls you a robber, my friend? Who calls you a thief?
All around the robbers beat their drums and thieves rule.
Who is the Daniel that sits in judgement over thieves and robbers?
Is there any in the world that is not an exploiter?

O Supreme judge, hold high your scepter,

For the great are great today only by robbing the weak.

The greater the robbery and theft, the cheating and the exploitation

The higher the status in the modern world of nations!

Palaces rise built with the congealed blood of subject peoples,

Capitalists run their factories by destroying a million hearths.

What diabolical machine is fed by human flesh?

Live men and women go in but come out like pressed sugar cane.

The factories squeeze the manhood out of millions,

And fill the millionaire's cup of wine and jars of gold.

The money lender grows potbellied on the food that the hungry need,

The landlord ruins the poor's home to drive his coach and four.

The merchant mind has turned the world into a brothel house,

Sin and Satan are its cup bearers and sing a song of greed.

Man has lost food and health and life and hope and speech,

Bankrupt, he rushes toward secure destruction.

There is hardly any way of escape,

For all around are trenches dug by the greed of gold.

The whole world is a prison and robbers are the guards.

Thieves have their brotherhood, cheats their comradeship.

Who calls you a robber, my friend? Who says you steal?

You have only taken a few coins or cups,

But you have not stabbed man in the heart!

You are not inhuman though you may be a thief,

Like Ratnakar, you can still become Valmiki if only you meet a real man!

—*Kazi Nazrul Islam*

LEISURE

Boys swimming in a pond in Pirigatcha village.

LIVING IN A COUNTRY ranked as one of the poorest in the world, Bangladeshis have become adept at recognizing and enjoying the simple pleasures of life during their leisure hours.

A wedding or a birth in a village, for example, is always an occasion for relatives, friends, and neighbors to get together. Here they can eat, drink, catch up on the latest family news and happenings, and renew ties with one another. Similarly an outdoor musical drama or performance never fails to attract crowds eager for good entertainment.

Sports and games also offer hours of pleasure, especially for boys. An impromptu game of soccer requires only an empty plot of land and

A competition picking the best prize bulls draws an enthusiastic crowd of spectators.

111

a ball. Watching television, listening to the radio, and going to the movies are popular pastimes for those who can afford a television or radio set, or the price of a movie ticket.

SOCIALIZING

Men do a great deal of socializing in public places. After prayers at the mosque, men often visit a teashop and sit together, chatting and drinking sweet tea, for several hours. Women do most of their socializing in the courtyard of their home, while performing their household tasks. They may weave or prepare food while they chat and gossip. Women visit one another's homes as well.

Bangladeshis can be very generous hosts. No effort or expense is spared to demonstrate the esteem in which a guest is held, and a small meal is always given to guests. A hostess will even prepare a meal for visitors who drop in unexpectedly. Dinner guests may be asked to arrive at 8:00 P.M. so that they have time for conversation before the meal is served. For special dinner parties, hosts sometimes arrange musical entertainment.

Shopworkers taking a tea break in between work.

SPORTS AND GAMES

Sports and games are extremely popular in Bangladesh. Children can often be seen playing soccer or cricket in quiet village streets. Many people enjoy chess as a recreational and competitive activity. *Kabaddi* (KAH-bah-dee) is a popular, and physical, indigenous sport, in which teams of six try to capture members of the opposing team. But the most popular sport in Bangladesh is undoubtedly soccer, which is played and supported passionately. Cricket, badminton, field hockey, tennis, swimming, and track and field also have strong followings. Bangladesh has the 9th top cricket team in the world.

Bangladesh competes in many international sports events, including the Olympics, Commonwealth, Asian, and South Asian Federation games. Bangladesh was the South Asian Football Federation champion in soccer in 2003. More often, however, the act of participating at international events is already a source of pride and achievement for all Bangladeshis.

Soccer is a popular sport among Bangladeshis.

MOVIES, TELEVISION, AND RADIO

Movies are a popular form of entertainment in Bangladesh. The country has produced its own films since 1948; today more than 100 feature films are produced each year. The Bangladeshi film industry, popularly known as Dallywood (a combination of the words Dhaka and Hollywood), has been based in Bangladesh's capital, Dhaka, since 1956. Despite the fact that most are long melodramas about the struggle for independence with mediocre acting and production quality, the movies attract an enthusiastic audience. In recent years efforts have been made to improve standards, and a handful of directors from Bangladesh have attained critical acclaim for their outstanding work. Recently the Bangladeshi film industry has faced increased competition from foreign films, satellite TV, home video, and other sources.

Banner promoting a movie in Chittagong.

Economic growth has ensured that television ownership has risen dramatically. In urban areas, 78 percent of households own a television set; in rural places, 27 percent own televisions. Twenty-five percent of households enjoy satellite television. Television viewership in 2004 was 64 percent, and recent years have seen an upsurge in Bangladeshi television channels. Many Bangladeshis also enjoy listening to the radio, but only a minority of people own radios—32 percent. A number of stations play music of varying styles, and read passages from the Koran and other scriptures. There is also a British Broadcasting Corporation (BBC) Bangla radio station.

A Bangladeshi boy finds some time to play with a homemade kite.

CHILDHOOD PURSUITS

Like their counterparts the world over, Bangladeshi children have little difficulty finding ways to amuse themselves. Simple toys can be made using whatever material is available and games can be as basic as hide-and-seek. Sports are also popular with many older children.

Yet many Bangladeshi children have little time to play. Young girls who do not attend school are put to work in the home, helping their mother and other female relatives with the household chores. Many children from poor families are also sent to work in factories and markets or placed in other employment to earn vital income to support their parents and siblings. Such work is often poorly paid, with long hours and tough working conditions.

FESTIVALS

Hindu devotees throwing bananas onto the chariot carrying
the deity Jagannath during Rathmela (Chariot Festival).

>A LTHOUGH MOST BANGLADESHIS
are Muslim and generally observe
Islamic holidays, Hindu, Buddhist, and
Christian festivals, as well as secular events,
are also celebrated.

MUSLIM FESTIVALS

Perhaps the most important event on the Islamic calendar is Ramadan,
the period of fasting. Although Ramadan is not a festival in the true
sense, the *iftar* (IF-tah) celebrations that go on in the evenings when the
fast is broken have all the attributes of a festival. Two weeks before
the beginning of Ramadan, alms and sweets are given to the poor.

Spectators at the Dhaka stadium await the start of the next event on the Victory Day
program of festivities.

Many festivals
celebrated in
Bangladesh
are religious in
nature. Ramadan,
which marks the
end of the Muslim
month of fasting,
is one of the
most important
festivals. Hindus
celebrate the
Festival of
Colors. Christians
celebrate
Christmas,
and Buddhists
celebrate the
birth of the
Buddha. Secular
festivals are
also celebrated
and center
mainly around
the nation's
independence.

A number of rules must be observed during Ramadan. Certain acts nullify the fast; if a person breaks the fast by performing one of these acts, he or she must make up for the lost time. Actions that nullify the fast include:

- Eating or drinking intentionally between dawn and dusk. If a Muslim eats or drinks unintentionally, forgetting that he or she is fasting, it is forgiven because it is said that Allah gave the food or drink to the person.

- Sexual intercourse

- Intentional vomiting

- Injections containing nourishment (unless used for medical purposes)

- Poor intentions—for example, intending to break the fast or not intending to start is considered as sin, even if the intention is not acted on.

- Involuntary actions, such as bleeding due to menstruation or childbirth

Eid al-Fitr (ID al-FIT-er) is a three-day festival celebrated immediately after the end of Ramadan. Bangladeshis eat special foods and socialize all night long. Most schools, shops, and offices are closed during the festival, and many people take vacation trips.

OTHER RELIGIOUS FESTIVALS

Hindus celebrate the festival of colors at the beginning of March. During this festival the participants throw colored water and powder on one another, and caste and social restrictions on both men and women are momentarily ignored.

The festival for Durga Puja (DERG-ah POO-jah), a Hindu goddess, is celebrated in October. Statues of the goddess riding a lion, with her 10 hands holding 10 different weapons, are placed in Hindu temples.

Bangladeshi women greet each other by applying *Sindoor* (an indication of married women) to their faces on the final day of Durga Puja, an annual Hindu festival that involves worship of the goddess Durga.

Buddhists celebrate the birth of the Buddha, and Christians celebrate Christmas and Easter.

SECULAR EVENTS

SHAHEED DIBOSH (MARTYRS' DAY) Celebrated on February 21 this day commemorates the death of four martyrs who were killed when Pakistani police opened fire on a procession protesting the decision to make Urdu the national language of East and West Pakistan.

INDEPENDENCE DAY Bangladesh declared its independence from Pakistan on March 26, 1971, sparking off a nine-month war. Independence Day celebrates the Bangladeshis' fight for independence.

Bangladeshi musicians perform during a parade celebrating the country's 35th Victory Day.

Muslim festivals fall on different dates each year because they are based on the Islamic lunar calendar. The following are some of the major religious and secular festivals celebrated in Bangladesh:

Martyrs' Day	*February 21*
Independence Day	*March 26*
Bengali New Year	*April 14*
May Day	*May 1*
Durga Puja	*October*
National Solidarity Day	*November 7*
Victory Day	*December 16*
Christmas	*December 25*
Eid al-Fitr	*varies*
Eid al-Azha	*varies*
Muharram	*varies*
Prophet Muhammad's Birthday	*varies*
The Buddha's Birthday	*varies*

The Bengali New Year is a time for new clothes and special cakes and sweets. Girls pick flowers to make garlands to wear around their neck and wrists.

BENGALI NEW YEAR This holiday falls on April 14.

BIJOY DIBOSH (VICTORY DAY) This festival celebrates the day when Bangladesh was finally liberated from Pakistan. Victory Day, December 16, marks the end of the war of independence and the birth of Bangladesh as a free nation.

FOOD

A fruit stall in Dhaka.

T HE CUISINE OF BANGLADESH, like that of its neighbors on the Indian subcontinent, has been influenced by the many conquerors who have passed through the land over the centuries. As a result the cuisine that has evolved is representative of the South Asian region.

The Mughal rulers have left perhaps the most lasting impression, and even today some of Bangladesh's food is derived from this heritage. The most visible examples of such food include kebabs (chunks of meat marinated in spices and grilled on skewers) and *koftas* (KOF-tahs,

Dosa, a paper-thin flat bread, is popular with Bangladeshis.

meatballs). These foods are also common to Iran and northern India, regions that were once part of the extensive Mogul Empire that reached its peak during the 17th century.

RICE

Rice is the staple of the Bangladeshi diet and is served with almost every meal. Poor people eat just plain rice with salt and pepper. The rice is prepared by boiling or frying in butter or oil. When there is a shortage of rice, the people will eat gruel or, reluctantly, wheat as a substitute.

Fish is a common side dish and provides most of the protein in the Bangladeshi diet. Meat, on the other hand, is reserved almost exclusively for festive occasions. Cattle, deer, goat, and chicken are commonly eaten. Every edible part of the animal is used, including the organs, and bones are boiled for stock. Domestic animals are the main source of meat, but these may be supplemented with hunted animals, such as wood pigeons, wild boars, iguanas, and large cats.

A rice dealer. Rice is a staple of the Bangladeshi diet.

FRUIT AND VEGETABLES

A wide variety of tropical fruit grows bountifully in Bangladesh. Mangoes, jackfruit, coconuts, bananas, and many other fruits are eaten fresh or form the basis of desserts. The availability of some fruit varies seasonally, but bananas, jackfruit, and papayas are almost always available in low-lying villages. Mandarin oranges are also becoming more common in the markets.

Wild limes, which grow in the hills, are a favorite among Bangladeshis. Most homes in the countryside have gardens that yield a ready supply of fresh vegetables for the family. In between harvests, leaves and roots, such as bamboo shoots and banana stalks, are gathered from the wild for the cooking pot.

MEALS

Breakfast is served very early, particularly in Muslim families. Men get up at dawn to pray, while the women prepare a breakfast of rice and milk and

A man buying starfruit.

perhaps some fruit. A fairly large lunch is eaten at midday, before the sun gets too hot.

The first time that the family is able to relax together is at the evening meal, which is usually served quite late, at 9:30 or 10:00 P.M. The family gathers on the veranda and sits on a bamboo mat, usually on the floor. The mother of the household serves food on individual plates to everybody. The meal does not begin until everyone has washed their hands. The evening meal usually consists of rice, spicy lentil, or dal (a dried legume), vegetables, and a little fish.

KITCHENS

Rural *baris* usually have a small shed that is not as well built as a sleeping room. This is designated as the kitchen. An interesting feature of Bangladeshi kitchens is the stove, which is built into the mud floor. Even in the more

A family in Char Kukri Mukri having a meal together.

affluent homes with brick walls and cement floors for the other rooms, the kitchen retains the mud floor. There may also be a built-in mud stove in the courtyard for open-air cooking during fair weather.

Cooking utensils quickly become covered in soot from the stoves, so they need to be cleaned regularly by rubbing them with ash and coconut husks. Utensils that are found in most kitchens include a grinding stone, round-bottomed earthenware pots, a winnowing basket, and a curved cutting edge fixed to a wooden base. Only very wealthy homes can afford kitchens equipped with modern appliances such as microwave ovens.

FORBIDDEN FOODS

The Bangladeshi diet has been influenced by the restrictions of the country's main religions. Muslims, for example, do not consume pork or alcohol, which

Mandi women cooking for a large gathering in their village.

are forbidden under Islam. Similarly Hindu Bangladeshis do not eat beef, as the cow is considered a sacred animal according to Hindu teachings. The relative absence of alcoholic beverages means that Bangladesh is very much a country of soft drinks, with Pepsi and Coca-Cola commonly seen even in the villages.

INTERNATIONAL FOODS

A modest variety of international cuisines, including Western food, can be found at major hotels and restaurants in the larger cities. In addition to several Chinese restaurants, Dhaka has Thai, Korean, Vietnamese, and Japanese restaurants.

Hindus deeply revere cows and abstain from eating them.

Bangladeshi cuisine is a generic term used to refer to the cooking style and trend now prevalent in Bangladesh. However, there are several regional variations.

Barisal, Chittagong, and Khulna, being close to the sea, tend to have a larger use of fish in their cuisines, in addition to coconut milk. Shutki, *which is a specially treated dry fish, is extremely popular in these areas. Chittagong also exports* shutki.

As a cosmopolitan city that has historically been the capital under Persio-Arabic rulers, Dhaka exhibits a great deal of Western influence in its cuisine. Dishes involving fried rice and a lot of meat are usually legacies of Dhaka's past as the capital of Bengali empires.

The west and northwest have, until recently, been untouched by the fashions and trends in the capital, Dhaka. As a result the high level of Persio-Arabic influence in the cuisine in and around Dhaka area is less pervasive here. Vegetable curries are the main dishes in these areas. Spices are also more commonly used.

The large number of lakes around the Sylhet division encourages greater use of lake fish in the cuisine. Because of the proximity to the hills in Assam, several fruits and pickles that are otherwise absent in rest of the country, such as satkorhai, *are used in cooking and serving.*

BENGALI CABBAGE CURRY

1 pound (0.45 kg) cabbage,
   sliced finely

2 potatoes, cut in small cubes

2 tablespoons (30 ml) oil

1 tablespoon (15 ml) turmeric

1¼ to 2 teaspoons (18.75—30 ml)
   green chili paste

1 tablespoon (15 ml) cumin, ground

1 tablespoon (15 ml) coriander,
   ground

1 inch (2.54 cm) grated ginger

1 tablespoon (15 ml) butter

2 bay leaves

½ teaspoon (7.5 ml) *garam masala*

Salt to taste

Sugar to taste

Fry cubed potatoes in hot oil in a wok until lightly browned. Remove the potatoes from oil and keep it aside. To the hot oil, add cabbage. Sprinkle with salt. Stir and cover. Simmer for 3 to 4 minutes. Remove cover. Add the turmeric, chili paste, cumin, coriander, and ginger. Stir and fry until the spices are well blended with the cabbage. The cabbage should be nearly cooked at this stage. Add ½ cup water (125 ml) and potatoes. Add salt and sugar to taste. Simmer over medium heat until potatoes are cooked and there is practically no gravy in the pan. In a frying pan, heat butter. Add the bay leaves and *garam masala*. Stir fry a couple of minutes and pour over the cabbage curry. Stir and remove from heat.

MISHTI DOI (SWEETENED YOGURT)

33.8 ounces (1 liter) full cream/whole milk

3—4 tablespoons (40—60 ml) yogurt

8.8 ounces (250 g) sugar

Boil the milk in a heavy-bottomed pan over a medium flame until it is reduced to half its original volume. Stir frequently to prevent the milk from scorching. When done, cool the milk until it is just lukewarm.

Put the sugar in another pan and heat over a low flame to melt. Allow the sugar to brown. Remove from the fire when done. Add the reduced milk to this browned sugar and mix well to blend.

When the milk and sugar are thoroughly mixed, add the yogurt to the mixture and stir gently to mix.

Pour into the desired container and keep in a warm dark spot for the Mishti Doi to set. The best results are achieved by setting the Mishti Doi in an earthenware pot.

When the Mishti Doi has set and has become firm, chill for a few hours and serve.

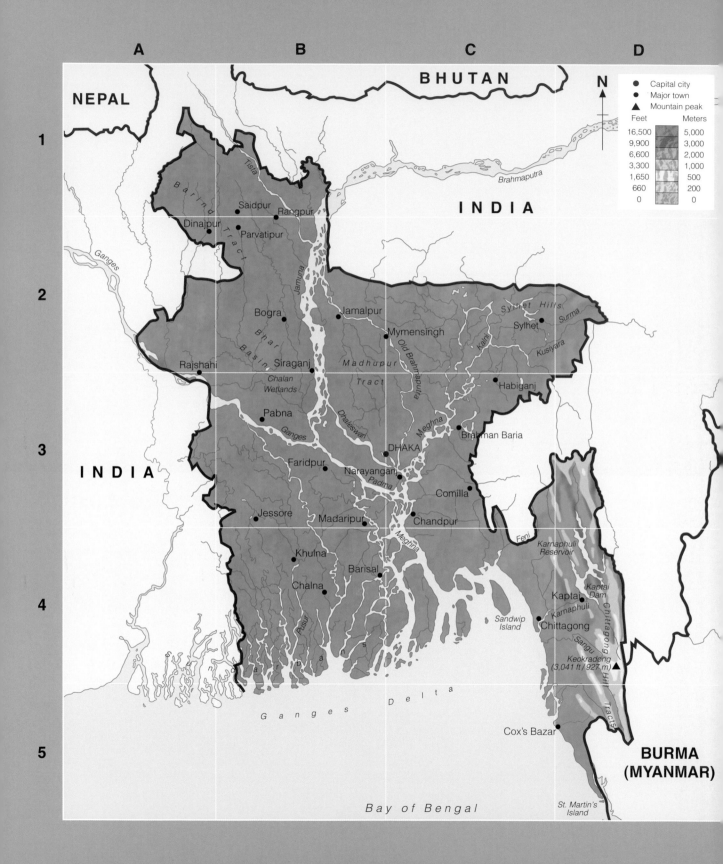

MAP OF BANGLADESH

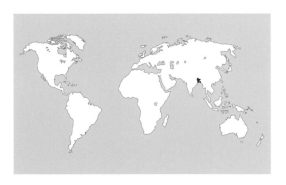

ECONOMIC BANGLADESH

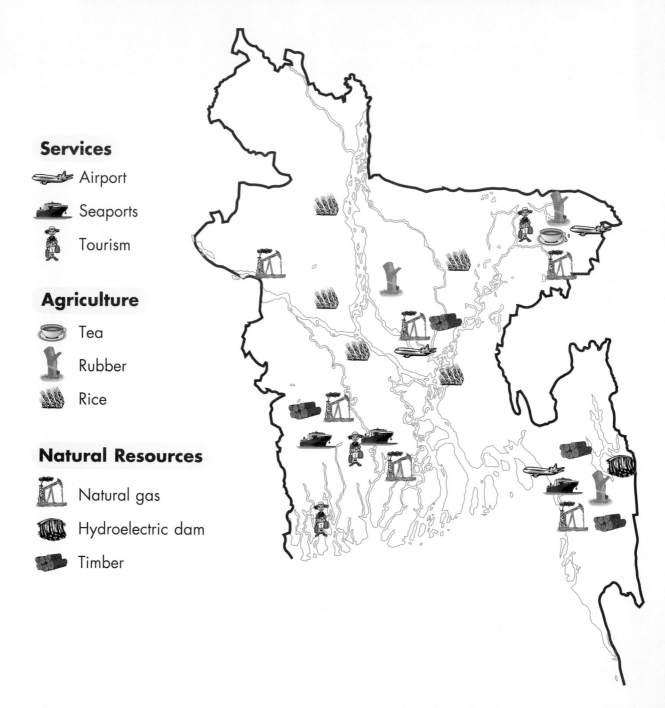

Services
- Airport
- Seaports
- Tourism

Agriculture
- Tea
- Rubber
- Rice

Natural Resources
- Natural gas
- Hydroelectric dam
- Timber

ABOUT THE ECONOMY

OVERVIEW

Bangladesh was ranked as the 48th-largest economy in the world by the International Monetary Fund in 2007. The economy has grown 6 to 7 percent annually over the past few years despite experiencing many difficulties. Bangladesh remains a poor, overpopulated, and inefficiently governed nation. Although more than half of the GDP is generated through the service sector, nearly two-thirds of Bangladeshis are employed in the agriculture sector, with rice as the single most important product. Garment exports and remittances from Bangladeshis working overseas, mainly in the Middle East and East Asia, fuel economic growth. Although it is one of the world's poorest and most densely populated countries, Bangladesh has made major strides to meet the food needs of its increasing population.

GROSS DOMESTIC PRODUCT (GDP)

US $208.3 billion (2007 estimate)

GDP GROWTH

6.3 percent (2007 estimate)

CURRENCY

Taka (BDT)
1 US$ = 68.8 Taka (November 2008)

LAND USE

Arable land: 55.39 percent, Permanent crops: 3.08 percent, Others: 41.53 percent

NATURAL RESOURCES

Natural gas, arable land, timber, and coal

AGRICULTURAL PRODUCTS

Rice, jute, tea, wheat, sugarcane, potatoes, tobacco, pulses, oilseeds, spices, fruit, beef, milk, and poultry

MAJOR EXPORTS

Garments, jute and jute goods, leather, frozen fish, and seafood

MAJOR IMPORTS

Machinery and equipment, chemicals, iron and steel, textiles, foodstuffs, petroleum products, cement

MAIN TRADE PARTNERS

United States, Germany, United Kingdom, France, China, India, Kuwait, and Singapore

WORKFORCE

69.4 million (2007 estimate)

UNEMPLOYMENT RATE

2.5 percent (2007 estimate)

INFLATION

9.1 percent (2007 estimate)

EXTERNAL DEBT

$21.23 billion (December 31, 2007 estimate)

CULTURAL BANGLADESH

Mahasthangarh Bogra
Mahasthangarh is the oldest archaeological site in Bangladesh on the western bank of the Karotoa River. The spectacular site is a fortified long enclosure. Several isolated mounds surround the fortified city. This is a sanctified site to the Hindus.

National Museum of Dhaka
This museum at Shahbag contains a number of collections including sculptures and paintings of the Hindu, Buddhist, and Muslim periods as well as inscriptions of the Koran in Arabic, and Persian letters and Bengali works in the Arabic script.

Jatiya Sangsad Bhaban
Jatiya Sangsad Bhaban (The National Parliament Building) is designed by the famous architect Louis I Kahn and known throughout the region for its architectural features. The main building is surrounded by a lake which also doubles as a reflecting pool.

Sundarbans
The Sundarbans is an area of 2,317 square miles (6,000 sq km) of swamps and mangrove forest along the coastal belt of Khulna. It is home to the royal Bengal tiger and other wildlife such as cheetahs and spotted deer.

Kantajee's Temple
Kantajee's Temple is the most ornate among the late medieval temples of Bangladesh. The temple rests on a slightly curved raised base of sandstone blocks, which are believed to have been quarried from the ruins of the ancient city of Bangarh.

Kuakata
Kuakata is a scenic beautiful spot on the southernmost tip of Bangladesh. Its beaches are also a sanctuary for migratory winter birds. Hindus and Buddhists take holy baths in the waters during their religious holidays.

Cox's Bazar
Cox's Bazar is the tourist capital of Bangladesh. It has the world's longest unbroken beach sloping gently down to the waters of the Bay of Bengal against the picturesque background of a chain of hills covered with deep green forests.

Sylhet
Sylhet is known as the "land of two leaves and a bud." It has terraced tea gardens, the colorful Khasia and Monipuri tribes, and exotic flora and fauna. It also has Jaintia, the ancient kingdom, and Madhabkunda, the famous waterfall.

Paharpur
Paharpur has been declared a World Heritage site by UNESCO, as the remains of the largest known monastery south of the Himalayas has been excavated there. This 8 A.D. archaeological find covers an area of 27 acres (11 hectares) of land.

Mainamati-Lamai range
The Mainamati-Lamai range is a range of hills dotted with more than 50 ancient Buddhist settlements. The Mainamati site Museum has a rich and varied collection of copper plates, gold and silver coins, and 86 bronze objects.

Kaptai
Kaptai is famous for its hydroelectric dam. It has a panoramic man-made 262 square mile (678.6 sq km) lake surrounded by hills and tropical forest. The Chit Morong Buddhist temple is only 1.86 miles (3 km) from Kaptai and it has beautiful Buddhist statues.

ABOUT THE CULTURE

OFFICIAL NAME
People's Republic of Bangladesh

FLAG DESCRIPTION
The Bangladesh flag features a red disk on a green background.

TOTAL AREA
55,598.7 square miles (144,000 sq km)

CAPITAL
Dhaka

ETHNIC GROUPS
Bengali 98 percent, Other 2 percent (includes tribal groups and non-Bengali Muslims)

RELIGION
Muslim 83 percent, Hindu 16 percent, Others 1 percent

BIRTHRATE
28.86 births per 1,000 (2008 estimate)

DEATH RATE
8 deaths per 1,000 (2008 estimate)

AGE STRUCTURE
0—14 years: 33.4 percent
15—64 years: 63.1 percent
65 years and over: 3.5 percent (2008 estimates)

MAIN LANGUAGES
Bangla (official, also known as Bengali), English

LITERACY
People age 15 and above, who can both read and write: 43.1 percent

LEADERS IN POLITICS
Khaleda Zia, Prime Minister (1991—96)
Habibur Rahman, Chief Advisor (1996)
Hasina Wazed, Prime Minister (1996—2001)
Latifur Rahman, Chief Advisor (2001)
Khaleda Zia, Prime Minister (2001—06)
Iajuddin Ahmed, Chief Advisor/President (2006—)
Fakhruddin Ahmed, Chief Advisor (2007—09)
Hasina Wazed, Prime Minister (2009—)

TIME LINE

IN BANGLADESH	IN THE WORLD
	323 B.C. Alexander the Great's empire stretches from Greece to India.
	1206–1368 Genghis Khan unifies the Mongols and starts a conquest of the world. At its height, the Mongol Empire under Kublai Khan stretches from China to Persia and parts of Europe and Russia.
	1789–99 The French Revolution
	1914 World War I begins.
	1939 World War II begins.
	1945 The United States drops atomic bombs on Hiroshima and Nagasaki.
1947 British colonial rule ends. A largely Muslim state consisting of East and West Pakistan is established.	
1949 The Awami League is established.	
1970 The Awami League wins an overwhelming election victory in East Pakistan.	
1971 Awami League leader Sheikh Mujib arrested and taken to West Pakistan. East Pakistan proclaims independence and renames itself Bangladesh.	
1972 Sheikh Mujib returns and becomes prime minister.	
1975 Sheikh Mujib becomes president of Bangladesh. He is assassinated in a military coup.	

IN BANGLADESH	IN THE WORLD

1977
General Zia Rahman assumes the presidency. Islam is adopted in the constitution.

1982
General Ershad assumes power in an army coup. He becomes president the following year.

1986
Nuclear power disaster at Chernobyl in Ukraine.

1988
Islam becomes the state religion.

1990
Ershad steps down following mass protests.

1991
Begum Khaleda Zia becomes prime minister.

1996
Sheikh Hasina Wajed becomes prime minister.

1997
Hong Kong is returned to China.

2000
Tensions between Bangladesh and Pakistan begin to escalate.

2001
Hasina steps down, hands the responsibility of power to the caretaker authority.

2003
War in Iraq begins.

2006
President Ahmed assumes caretaker role for period leading to elections.

2007
A state of emergency is declared amid violence in the election run-up. Elections are postponed.

2008
An alliance headed by Sheikh Hasina wins 50 out of 65 seats in the 300-seat parliament, according to unofficial first results.

GLOSSARY

akht (AHKT)
Legal declaration of marriage in Islamic tradition

bari (BAH-ree)
Rural Bangladeshi home

chakras
Centers of energy in the body

dal
A dried legume

dhole (DOL)
Country drum, a common village instrument

esraj (EHZ-rahj)
Traditional Bengali instrument

goli (GOH-lee)
Area in the home used by men for socializing

Hadith
Collection of the Prophet Muhammed's sayings

iftar (IF-tah)
Celebrations that go on in the evenings when the fast is broken during Ramadan

jatra (JA-trah)
Village folk play

Kaaba
Building covered in black cloth that stands in the courtyard of the Great Mosque

Kabaddi (KAH-bah-dee)
Popular and physical indigenous sport in which teams of six players try to capture members of the opposing team

kirtan (KEER-tahn)
Prayer dance to worship God

kobul (koh-BUL)
I accept

lungi (LOONG-gee)
Sarong-like cloth worn by men

mullah
Learned man

namaste (NAHM-ahst-ay)
Standard greeting among Hindus

purdah
Regulating code of behavior for woman where she conducts herself modestly in the presence of adult males

Ramadan
Period of fasting required of all Muslims

salat (sah-LAHT)
Daily prayer, five times a day, by Muslims

sawm (soom)
Fast during Ramadan

shagatom (SHAH-gah-tom)
"Welcome" in Bengali

sitar
Classical Indian stringed instrument

zakat (zah-KAHT)
The giving of alms to the poor

FOR FURTHER INFORMATION

BOOKS

Brooks, Susie. *Bangladesh: In the Children's Own Words* (Our Lives, Our World). London: Chrysalis Children's Books, 2004.

Gritzner, Charles F. *Bangladesh* (Modern World Nations). New York: Chelsea House Publishers, 2007.

London, Ellen. *Bangladesh* (Countries of the World). Singapore: Times Editions, 2004.

March, Michael. *Bangladesh* (Country Files). London: Franklin Watts, 2004.

Orr, Tamara B. *Bangladesh* (Enchantment of the World, Second Series). New York: Children's Press, 2007.

Price, Khojesta A. *Tales from Bangladesh*. Trafford Publishing, 2006.

Streissguth, Tom. *Bangladesh in Pictures* (Visual Geography. Second Series). Minneapolis, MN: Twenty-First Century Books, 2008.

Thomson, Ruth. *Bangladesh* (Living in). London: Franklin Watts Ltd, 2005.

Valliant, Doris. *Bangladesh* (The Growth and Influence of Islam in the Nations of Asia and Central Asia). Philadelphia, PA: Mason Crest Publishers, 2005.

WEBSITES

www.banglapedia.org/english/

The Bangladesh Channel. www.bangladesh.com/

National Web Portal of Bangladesh. www.virtualbangladesh.com/

News From Bangladesh. http://newsfrombangladesh.net/

Virtual Bangladesh. www.virtualbangladesh.com/

FILMS

Masud, Tareque, and Masud Catherine. *A Kind of Childhood—Child Labor in Bangladesh*. Direct Cinema Limited, DVD, 2007.

Swimmer, Saul. *The Concert for Bangladesh* (Limited Deluxe Edition). Rhino Records, DVD, 2005.

MUSIC

Bloomsburg to Bangladesh: *Bloomsburg to Bangladesh*. Blue Buddha Records, 2004.

George Harrison: *The Concert for Bangladesh*. Capitol, 2005.

Various Artists: *Echoes from Bangladesh*. Fremeaux & Assoc. Fr , 2003.

BIBLIOGRAPHY

BOOKS

Abdul, Awal Mintoo. *Bangladesh: Anatomy of Change*. Athena Press Publishing Co. UK, 2006.

Banu, U.A.B. Razia Akter. *Islam in Bangladesh*. New York: Leiden, 1992.

Bonapace, Laura. *Diggin' Dhaka* (Map). Bonapace Associates, 2008.

Butler, Stuart. *Bangladesh* (Country Guide). Lonely Planet, 2008.

Chakravarti, S. R., & Narain, Virendra. *Bangladesh*. New Dehli: South Asian Publishers, 1986.

ITMB Publishing. *Bangladesh Map by ITMB* (Travel Reference Map). ITMB Publishing, 2003.

Karlekar, Hiranmay. *Bangladesh: The Next Afghanistan?* New Delhi ; Thousand Oaks, Calif. : Sage Publications SAGE Publications, 2006.

Novak, James J. *Reflections on the Water*. Bloomington: Indiana University Press, 1993.

Riaz, Ali. *God Willing: The Politics of Islamism in Bangladesh*. Rowman & Littlefield Publishers, 2004.

The Chittagong Hill Tracts: Militarization, Oppression and the Hill Tribes. London: Anti-Slavery Society, 1984.

Trenowden, Mark. *Expatriate Games—662 days in Bangladesh*. Derwent Press, 2005.

West Asia on a Shoestring. Victoria, Australia: Lonely Planet Publications, 1990.

Yunus, Muhammad. *Banker To The Poor: Micro-Lending and the Battle Against World Poverty*. New York: PublicAffairs, 2003.

WEBSITES

BBC News: Country profile: Bangladesh. http://news.bbc.co.uk/2/hi/south_asia/country_profiles/1160598.stm

BBC News: Science: Nature: UK gives Bangladesh climate help. http://news.bbc.co.uk/2/hi/science/nature/7606024.stm

Dhaka newspapers: Dhaka newspaper list. www.newspapers24.com/world-cities/dhaka-newspapers/

Emerald: Article Request: Closing the gender gap in Bangladesh: inequality in education, employment and earnings. www.emeraldinsight.com/Insight/viewContentItem.do?contentType=Article&contentId=1463176

Illegal Fishing Information—Bangladesh. www.illegal-fishing.info/sub_approach.php?country_title=bangladesh

Nation Master. www.nationmaster.com/index.php

Post-Imperial English Status Change. http://books.google.co.nz/books?id=SIu244rlVu8C&pg=PA63&lpg=PA63&dq=circulation+of+daily+tribune+-+khulna&source=bl&ots=FTY5DkCanO&sig=pBsYvxJ7EcXb5dAQD4DKyLvoGtY&hl=zh-CN&sa=X&oi=book_result&resnum=2&ct=result#PPA63,M1

South Asia: Gender and Social Transformation in Bangladesh. http://web.worldbank.org/WBSITE/EXTERNAL/COUNTRIES/SOUTHASIAEXT/0,,contentMDK:21685068~pagePK:146736~piPK:146830~theSitePK:223547,00.html

INDEX

INDEX